Cedar Hill Publications

The Heat

*Steelworker
Lives & Legends*

Cover Art: Detail of the Stained Glass Memorial at United
Steelworkers of America Headquarters in Pittsburgh featuring
Joe Magarac, the mythical steelworker, who was so obsessed with
making perfect steel that he threw himself in a molten cauldron.
The Memorial commemorates those who work in the mills and
those who died making steel. Designed by Richard Collavo, Jim
Haley, Wayne Hanbury, Dave McConaha, George McDonald,
John Sigmund, and Bill Steele. Photograph by Tom Fitzpatrick.
Courtesy Visual Perceptions Inc.

Distribution: *Institute for Career Development*
                    888/291-8003 Toll Free
                    Borders.com
                    Barnes & Noble.com

Manufactured in the United States of America

Printed by: *Bang Printing*
                  Brainerd, Minnesota
                  800/328-0450
                  Equal Opportunity Employer/Contractor

Cedar Hill Publications
3722 Hwy. 8 West
Mena, Arkansas 71953

Contents

Preface
George Becker

Foreword
Harmon Lisnow

Introduction
Jimmy Santiago Baca

SECTION I: Hiring In

A New Pair of Boots — *Bill Corrigan* 17
Remembering What's Important — *Kathi Wellington Dukes* 21
Day One — *Jennifer Jones* 27
Going to the Mill — *Gary Novotny* 31

SECTION II: The Way It Was

History of the Union Part I:
    From An Inferno — *Marty Marciniak* 35
The Card — *Kathi Wellington Dukes* 36
Hey Johnny! I Got My SWOC Button — *Marty Marciniak* 39
Company Town — *Sandy Dunn* 47

SECTION III: Workers We Knew

Hawkeye — *Joe E. Gutierrez* .55
Scottie — *Jerry Ernest* 59
Thunderbird — *Chuck Canty* .63
Wild Bill — *Stan Daniloski* 65
Ma Beth — *Kathi Wellington Dukes* 69

Section IV: Family

Darcy and the Silly Men — *Gary Markley* 73

Men of Steel, Hearts of Gold — *P. David Woodring* 90

The Watch — *J.A. Orellana* 97

Alan Kepler — *Joe E. Gutierrez* 98

Steelworker Talking Thoughts — *Gary Novotny* 101

Long Live 'D' Crew — *Gary Markley* 103

Deliverance — *Wendy Marciniak* 117

Section V: The Cost of Steel

History of the Union Part II:
  Rolling Along the Line — *Marty Marciniak* 121

Snow Danced in August — *Joe Gutierrez* 122

Leftovers — *Chuck Canty* 125

Don't Mind the Noise — *J.A. Orellana* 128

Women in the Mill — *Jennifer Jones* 129

The Union's Best Friend — *Joe Lunchbox* 139

Dear Lisa — *Norman T. Brown, Jr.* 132

Section VI: The Finishing End

History of the Union Part III:
  Cobbled and Hobbled — *Marty Marciniak* 137

Little Joe — *Joe E. Gutierrez* 130

Who the Hell Are You? — *Gary Markley* 145

Outside Looking In — *J.A. Orellana* 151

Missing At Work — *Joe E. Gutierrez* 152

A Violet in the Light — *Dwight "Doc" Iler* 154

Preface

This book is about the American Dream. Not the '90s version of making millions by investing in the right Internet startup, but the old-fashioned American Dream of working hard, paying your dues and pulling yourself up by your bootstraps to make a decent living for your family.

This country has changed a lot in the last 50 years and the Steelworkers have had to change with it. Once upon a time, a job in the steel mills was considered a secure job, perhaps for a lifetime. The mills offered thousands of American men and women both security and excellent wages. A job in the mill meant a steady paycheck for 30 years and the opportunity to retire with a full pension.

"A good meal ticket for the price of 10 years off your life." That's how J.A. Orellana describes mill work in a poem he contributed to this book. That's a pretty good description. It's tough, demanding work, with no room for error. While their union has fought hard to make working conditions safer, workers' lives are put in jeopardy every day. But their union couldn't stop the biggest threat Steelworkers ever faced: the near-collapse of the steel industry in the 1980s.

It was a brutal decade. America lost close to eight million industrial jobs in the 1980s. Imports, downsizing and an industry-wide corporate restructuring eliminated 350,000 Steelworker jobs. In many respects, the devastation was so concentrated within these communities that our members became virtually unemployable; there were simply no jobs to be had.

Compounding the problem was the fact that the workers' skills were so specific to the jobs they performed in the mills that they couldn't be applied to other sectors of the job market. This left Steelworkers dead in their tracks. That's when we hit on the idea for the Institute for Career Development. We negotiated with the steel companies to provide education and training that would give Steelworkers a chance to develop the skills they needed to stay competitive in the changing economy.

The Institute, or ICD, was created so that our members would never again face the fear and uncertainty of losing their jobs without having some marketable skills to back them up. It's a wonderful program that lets workers chart their own future. They decide on the curriculum. They take the classes they want. Some study computers. Others get college degrees. And many develop skills that lead to secondary careers as electricians or plumbers or air-conditioning repairmen. Basically, Steelworkers can use the program to develop a wide variety of skills.

This book is the product of a workshop that Steelworkers fashioned to develop their creative writing skills. It's a collection of stories and poems that reflect the culture of the mills. The mills are a microcosm of America, but they constitute a subculture rarely seen. Inside the mills, you'll find the full spectrum of human emotion: joy, despair, fear, pride, anger and kindness. Somehow, Steelworkers are able to transcend the dreary working conditions to find meaning in their lives. They are dignified people. They understand they made a choice. They bought into the middle-class American Dream—at once alienated by the mill and yet appreciating it for the jobs it provides. I'm proud of these writers for having the courage to share their stories with the reading public and for showing America what it means to be a Steelworker.

— *George F. Becker*
International President,
United Steelworkers of America—AFL-CIO/CLC

Foreword

What a journey! It started with an understanding that Steelworkers have strong experiences to write about. They also have the creative and intellectual ability to tell powerful stories. The writings in this marvelous book are filled with pain, anger, anguish and despair, but as the creative process unfolded, other aspects of Steelworker values, attitudes and culture emerged. With all the darkness and fury, there is also humor and a strong sense of camaraderie reflected in the deep, abiding friendships formed between "brothers and sisters" working in dangerous conditions. The book reflects, more than anything else, the transcendent ability of Steelworkers to overcome the tough environments of the mills and mines. Their stories show their ability to rise above the darkness and shed light on everything they do.

As much as they are angry about their work environments; as much as they feel captive to a way of life they sometimes despise; and as much as they resent how they're treated, Steelworkers recognize that they made a choice. The mills and mines gave them a way to provide a decent living for their families. This book reflects a high standard of commitment and loyalty. Given a choice between fighting to keep the steel industry competitive and vibrant, or leaving the world of steel, they have opted to put their lives on the line, "put in their time," and leave a legacy of survival.

As I came to know these Steelworker authors on a personal basis, I was awed by their ability to do so many things in their lives, and to do them well. But the most remarkable thing I witnessed was their spiritual growth. They evolved into leaders who learned to accept themselves and their conditions by giving to others. In many cases, this transformation was forged by their relationship with their union, the United Steelworkers of America.

These great stories, vignettes and poems give readers a truly astounding window into the much misunderstood culture of American labor, particularly the Steelworker experience. None of this would be possible without the incredible guiding hand of a true literary giant, poet and author,

Jimmy Santiago Baca. Jimmy's creative genius, combined with his pure writing ability, boundless compassion, iron will to do what's right, and the instincts of a street hustler, make for some dynamic teaching. He brought his great strengths to these Steelworker authors and elevated this collaboration by allowing them to write and write, wonderfully and honestly, from their hearts about their lives and experiences. Without Jimmy Baca's vision and determination, this book would just be a dream of frustrated Steelworkers and the ICD, rather than a published, seminal statement about the Steelworker reality.

Finally, I want to thank George Becker, International President of the USWA, and union co-chair of ICD, whose guiding hand and vision has made our program a successful reality. I also want to thank Peter Kelly, CEO and Chairman of the Board of LTV Steel Inc., and management co-chair of ICD, who is a friend of the program and was there when we needed him. The same sentiment of thanks goes to all Governing Board members, Advisory Board members, Local Joint Committee members and participating Steelworkers who collectively created the environment that allows our work to be successful. Without the continued support and cooperation of union and management there would be no program and no book.

Lynn Williams and Bernie Kleiman, your vision is a reality.

— *Harmon Lisnow*
ICD Executive Director

Introduction

Steelworkers from several mills took time from their busy lives to check out this poet who was going to be facilitating a writing workshop. Many of them worked overtime, double shifts, and graveyard shifts, so they had to juggle their schedules to fit in the workshop. It was not easy for them to give away the precious spare time they usually spent with their families.

In the past, they were betrayed by the distortion of themselves perpetuated by the national media and academia. For some, their stories and opinions were placed in a context that created something entirely different from what they originally meant. The first night of our workshop, I tried to assure them I was not going to deceive them. I told them that I hoped that their poems and stories would eventually be anthologized and that I had no inclination to abuse their trust to attain tenure-track or other academic brownie points.

My interest in leading a workshop stemmed from two experiences. The first was a brief introduction to a union man named Tony. He was a union man working on the docks in Chicago all his life, and when the doctor told him he had only a year to live, I moved my family from New Mexico to Florida to be at his side. During that year, I learned what a beautiful man he was: he had integrity, fearless truth, and a subdued humble love for his family. He would always tell me that had he the opportunity to change his life, he would have become a writer. He would have been a good one too. His opinions on national affairs sobered me with their clarity and thoughtfulness. And when I asked him where he learned all this, he said the union, working next to men and women fifty years, listening to them and discussing public matters with them.

One day, as his condition worsened, and when he was within weeks of dying, I asked him what singular and simple bit of advice he had to offer me. I was looking for something to guide my consciousness. His response was surprisingly simple. He said, "If you remember nothing else, know that no man has the right to oppress another."

My second experience was my second-hand encounter with Steelworkers. When I was reading at a university a few years ago, on the way back to my hotel, I asked the driver what that dark warehouse was to the left of us. It ran the length of the waterfront for miles and it looked formidable, ugly and menacing in the dusk, brooding in its own despair. My escort said it was a steel mill that had been shut down. I asked her to park so I could observe it more closely. For the next couple of hours, I walked alongside it in the dark, sensing a great tragedy, epic in proportion. I wondered what had happened to all the generations of people who had their history, culture and lives connected to this place— what happened to them? Where were they? What were the stories they had to tell? Certainly, what secrets they kept in their hearts was part of the American experience, and yet, after reading thousands of books over the past twenty-five years, I had never read anything written by Steelworkers.

This perplexed me and my consternation grew as I went walking through the neighborhood adjacent to the mill. It was falling apart. I saw people on doorsteps drinking. Young men out of work. Others walked past me with that pale, bloodless look on their face that told me they were on drugs. It was sad and unacceptable. I thought of how thousands of other people who had been shut out of the mills, had spiraled into alcoholism, drug abuse, poverty and permanent unemployment, but I also realized that when the mill had closed its door and closed off many lives, it had not, and could not, close off the memories or wipe away a lifetime of shared experiences.

The mill was a city where kids came in with dreams, and through arduous struggle and fearless honesty, grew to become men and women with integrity. The mill changed them—some got married and had families; others learned to sacrifice for their fellow workers; others changed significantly and became who they never thought they could. The mill may have chained and locked its doors, but in doing so, it brought forth a waterfall of memories shared around dinner tables, generations of stories told around the picnic table, on the porch, and during fishing trips.

And this was what the workshop had to do—it had to bring a small sampling of those stories to paper and then to a book so the public could read them and know their fellow Americans, the men and women who supplied the steel to build American cities.

When we got back into the car, I knew, as we rode past the rusting miles of steel, that their stories had to be told. Stories of dreams shattered. Faith kept intact through prayer. Aspirations. Struggle. Oppression. And somewhere in my heart, at that moment, I knew my fate would be to meet with the Steelworkers.

A few months later, I found myself talking with Harmon Lisnow, executive director of the Institute for Career Development, and his assistants Cindy and Andy. Harmon was immediately enthusiastic about starting up a writing workshop and he asked, looking directly into my eyes, "When?" We shared the same vision about publishing stories that shimmered like sunken ship treasures in the heart of Steelworkers, aching to rise into the light of day. He flew me out, put me in a hotel, gave me an office, and the writing workshop took off, with us meeting on alternating days and nights in that classroom/office in Merrillville, Indiana.

What developed are incredible stories and poems, as good or better than any short stories being published today. I say "better" because, while they are grounded in lived experience and painstakingly crafted, they also go a step further. It's that step that is indefinable and mysterious, that is the glimmering lure that appeals to the human heart, familiar to the soul, a lost relative back from a long journey who we thought we'd never see again. The stories and poems not only reclaim a spiritual piece of ourselves and carry something innate and important to our human makeup, but in some strange, inexplicable manner, brim an empty place in our hearts with a quiet joy equal to a newborn babe in its mother's arms. These stories and poems redefine our commitment to each other and community, and to our love for humanity in a way few anthologies do.

In closing, I want to thank Stacy James for her help with this anthology. She spent weeks in Merrillville, Indiana, at the ICD office working closely with individual steelworkers on their stories and poems. And she was indispensable in helping to facilitate the writing workshops. This anthology would not be the achievement that it is, had she not worked tirelessly going over and over the stories, reading and re-reading them, categorizing, organizing, and editing them. She is an astute and gifted editor, and this collection reflects the sincerity of her compassionate heart.

— *Jimmy Santiago Baca*

SECTION I: Hiring In

A New Pair of Boots

Bill Corrigan

The morning after my eighteenth birthday, I walked a mile to the Hessville bus stop to catch a ride to the steel mills. I was unemployed. A day earlier my father had asked, "Now what are you going to do?"

"I guess I'm going to the mills," I said.

Why not? Everybody else was. In the late '60s and early '70s the mills had high employee turnover and a job was pretty much guaranteed.

My car had just bitten the dust so I boarded the No. 2 bus and rode two hours through Hammond and East Chicago to Indiana Harbor—the mills.

When I arrived at the harbor section, I was lost. I had never been this close to Inland Steel before. The bus dropped me off at the huge No. 30 parking lot. A plant guard told me how to get to the employment office. I had to follow the employee walkway over the "ant hill," the only bridge leading to the Plant 2 mills. I learned later that many a man had been mugged and stabbed on the walkway, especially on payday.

I made it to the bottom of the walkway and could see the employment office on the corner, a block away. It was a one-story, dirty, soot-stained, brown brick building with fogged glass-block windows. The steel-framed glass door wheezed and whooshed as I opened it to enter. The place looked like an auto license branch. There was a long counter along one wall with divided openings, and in the center of the room there were three rows of plastic molded chairs. The walls were a two-tone, dentist-office green. The place was full of people standing at each opening of the counter. I weaved my way to the front and snatched an application.

I could hear the lady behind the counter asking a man if he could speak English. All he could do was smile and nod his head. She asked him about five times until she told him, "Don't come back until you learn a little bit of English."

I found an empty chair and filled out my application. I noticed a vacant spot at the counter, zoomed up there and slid my application across the counter to the lady who was having problems with non-English speakers all morning. She glanced at my application and told me to go through the door on the other side of the building, have a seat, and wait.

It was an office connected to the one I was just in. I waited a few minutes and a man in a suit walked in and called my name. I followed him to a beat-up wooden teacher's desk and took a seat on the chair next to it. He asked me what department I wanted to work in, but I knew nothing about the mill.

"You're going to No. 3 Open Hearth labor gang," he said. "Once you've made union, you can decide where to go."

I proceeded to sign about 20 cards and forms for reasons I still don't understand. Next I was directed to the clinic next door for a physical and blood and urine tests. They didn't test for drugs back then; they just hired heartbeats.

After the physical, I was sent across the street to the safety-shoe store to get my steel-toed work shoes. The store had a deep, tanned, leathery odor with a sweet tint of shoe polish. There were five other men in the store seated in molded plastic chairs trying on shoes. I approached an old gray-haired man behind the counter. His face was a dried-up granny apple with half of an unlit cigar sticking out of his mouth. His breath smelled like a pig took a crap in his mouth.

I slid my shoe card across the counter. He snatched it up, looked at me, and snarled, "Well?"

"I want some shoes," I said.

"No shit! What size and what kind do you want?" he said.

"Safety shoes," I replied.

"Go look at the shoe display in the glass counter and tell me the number of the fucking shoe you want!" he yelled.

I looked around and it appeared the other people had just received the same treatment I was getting. I finally found a pair of shoes to my liking. They were high-top, black leather, tractor-soled metatarsal boots with eight miles of leather shoe strings. Little did I know the pain I was in for breaking them in. A few minutes later a plant guard came in and ordered us into a dark-blue Chevy Suburban parked outside. We piled in and were on our way up and over the ant hill to the north gate and into the mill.

Looking out the window it hit me like a ton of bricks. I was scared shitless. I didn't realize how massive and filthy the mill was. I could see the line of smokestacks of No. 2 Open Hearth belching out red billowy dust-filled smoke into the air and onto the cars in lot No. 30, covering them with fine red powder and tinting the windows red and gray.

I was awestruck at the size of the buildings in the mill. They were all a hundred feet tall and ranged from a quarter-mile to a half-mile long. They were painted a rusty primer red. I didn't know what was in those buildings, but they were huge.

We pulled up to one of the quarter-mile-long buildings. The guard called my name. "This is No. 3 Open Hearth, pal. Go in there and find the labor office," he said as he pointed to a door.

I hopped out and he zoomed away with the other five people. Holding my boxed work shoes, I could smell the leather odor oozing out of the cardboard lid. I entered the building and found the labor office on the first floor. It was a meeting room with four rows of wooden benches. There I met the labor foreman. He looked like the evil military guy on Rocky & Bullwinkle. He was straightforward and told me about the starting and quitting time. That was it. He called in a labor pusher for my orientation, which consisted of getting a pair of safety glasses and a hard hat with white stripes indicating a new employee.

The labor pusher took me to the second-floor locker room and showed me an empty locker. "This is your locker. Do you have a lock for it?" he asked.

"No," I said.

"Too bad. Get your boots on. You're going to work," he told me.

What did I get myself into? I'm starved, I thought. *I'm not wearing work clothes. I can't work now!*

I was wearing blue jeans, a T-shirt, a light jacket and tennis shoes. I tried to explain to him, but it was no use. I kicked off my sneakers and put on the work boots. Man, were they stiff! I could hardly walk. I felt like Herman Munster with ankle weights.

There I was, in hard hat, goggles, work boots, and no gloves. I followed the pusher outside and down a long road that ran the entire length of the big red building. We stopped about halfway down the road, and he pointed to a set of stairs leading down to a basement. When I got down there, it wasn't a basement, but exhaust or flu tunnels from the furnaces to the smoke stacks. I spent the remaining three hours of the day shift shoveling red flu dust into a wheelbarrow and dumping it into a big metal box to be hoisted away.

The end of the shift came and I was covered from head to toe with red flu dust. I headed straight to the locker room and, sure enough, my shoes were gone. I just shook my head and washed up as best I could. I jumped on the cattle car to the north clock house and I caught the No. 2 bus back to Hessville.

Looking out the window of the bus as we crossed the ant hill, I said to myself, "Yep, I'm just gonna stay here til I find a better job."

That was 29 years ago.

Remembering What's Important
Kathi Wellington Dukes

Working as a skip tracer for a credit and collection agency in Gary, Indiana was depressing. I considered seeing a doctor for some kind of relief. There was only one thing that stopped me: the bruises all over my body from frequent battles with my husband. The fights became more violent as his gambling and drinking intensified. He only let me work so he could spend more of his mill paycheck on his own pleasures. I was only allowed to spend money on milk and the necessities for our son. His check was usually gone after the second day he cashed it.

One day a client came in to pay his debt and told me that he was going to apply at Bethlehem Steel. He had heard they were hiring two hundred workers. He said his previous mill experience would land him a position. I leaned over the counter, grabbed him by the shirt, and asked him where I could get an application.

Standing in the pouring rain at five o'clock in the morning, I watched as the crowd grew from several hundred to over a thousand. The thunder cracked violently and the lightning arced across the sky, but I didn't want to lose my place in line. As close as I could figure, there were fewer than a hundred people in front of me.

When they finally unlocked the door at seven o'clock, the crowd surged forward and everyone in front was smashed into a second locked door. A girl's purse caught on the edge of the door frame and she fell to her knees. She started screaming as people stepped on her to get inside. The mob swelled into the building. The personnel people explained that they were only going to hire two hundred. To calm the near-riot, the mill gave an application to everyone.

As I drove home, I thought about my husband's experience hiring on at the mill. In 1970 he had applied at three different mills and they called within a week asking him to take a physical. What a difference eight years had made in the economy.

The next four months were the lowest period of my life. My husband discovered my application. When I took it to the post office, I wore dark sunglasses to hide the shiner he had given me. He said that no wife of his was going to work in a steel mill with all those men.

I was determined to be the fourth generation in my family to work in the mill. I started target shooting with my father. The final thing that propelled my legs out the door of the collection agency was seeing my boss squeeze himself through his pants as he stared at me through the glass window of his office. The minimum wage made it easy to walk away.

As I pulled into the parking lot of my apartment, I saw a county marshal on the front steps. He was there to serve me divorce papers. I was surprised my husband beat me to the final punch. I had always pictured the scene quite differently, with me making a long speech followed by a dramatic exit. I had been replaced by a newer model.

I asked my mom to keep my son for the weekend and I drank myself into a coma. On Monday morning, the phone rang six times before I could focus enough to pick it up. It was the mill wanting me to come in and take a typing test and a physical. I told them I would be there in an hour. I ran to the bathroom, jammed my finger down my throat, cleared out my stomach, and jumped into the shower.

Four hours later I had passed the typing test and the physical. There was a God. My blood-alcohol level must have been over .2 percent.

The following Friday, I returned to the mill. They said there were no clerical positions at the time, but they would keep my record in the "active" file. As I reached for the door to leave, I asked her what positions they were filling at the time.

"Labor," was the woman's reply.

"Listen, lady," I said. "My husband just dumped me, I quit my job last Friday, and I have a five-year-old kid to feed. I'll shovel shit with a smile on my face. Please, just give me a break!"

"You can start Monday," she said without looking up.

I showed up an hour early and chain-smoked a half pack of cigarettes before the doors were unlocked at the employment office. Six other men were hired that same day. All of them were white except for Ray. Ray fell asleep during the safety videos and again during the paper-signing segment of the hiring process. Instead of asking Ray to leave, the instructor simply raised his voice to be heard over the raspy snoring. Ray and I were assigned to the plate mill. All the white boys went to the hot mill.

Ray was pleasantly surprised by his assignment. He thought he was going to end up in the coke ovens or the blast furnace. While we waited for the department trucks to pick us up, he explained to me how blacks were usually assigned the dirty side of the mill. He decided to wait and see before he considered himself lucky. Ray turned out to be smarter than he looked.

I squeezed in between two sub-foremen in the front of the truck while Ray jumped in back and nodded off. They took us for a ride around the entire mill and explained the workings of our department. After the tour was over, I crawled into the back and shook Ray awake. He had missed the roadside view of the dirty side of the mill. The plate mill seemed sparkly clean in comparison. He might not have felt lucky, but I did.

We filled out more paper work and read safety papers in the office. The rest of the crew came in and snuck a peek at the new workers. I quickly realized I was the only woman in the department. Other women had been there before me but quickly transferred after their probation period. The gang consisted of thirty-six white men and three black men, including Ray. There were two turn foremen and six sub-foremen—one black. The gang let me know within minutes that he was a snitching dog and that I should watch what I told him.

We were instructed to go downstairs and eat our lunch early. No one took their hard hats or glasses off. Ten minutes later I found out why. The "banana wars" broke out. The objective was simple and the result was gross. You chewed up your banana, spit it in your hand, and slung it at everyone in the room. They spared me the first day since I didn't have any ammunition, but recommended that I come armed the next morning. The men were all between 18 and 23 years old. It was hard to accept their junior-high mentality. I packed a banana in the morning, just the same.

The foreman came down and assigned the job of trash run to Ray, Jake and me. Jake was a human wall: six foot five, three hundred and fifty pounds. His skin was the color of India ink.

"Come on," was all he said. For the next three hours we walked over, under, around and through the three-quarters-of-a-mile-long building that constituted the plate mill. The sound of the plates moving down the endless roll line was deafening. The oily, dirty steam that filled the building felt like a sauna. Streams of sweat left clear trails on my face while the filthy steam coated my skin with a layer of tar.

There was no conversation as we followed Jake around. We started picking up on the sign language that was used to convey thoughts. We quickly learned to distinguish "white hat," which was indicated by tapping our helmet on top, from "crane overhead," which was pointing at the eye and then upward. The noise was so deafening in some spots that we couldn't hear the sirens as a load of steel passed overhead.

Working our way east through the building, the noise and heat subsided. The shipping end of the building was more tolerable, except for the frenzied pace of the crane operators. We stepped outside to unload the last of the garbage from our backs.

"Keep three light ones for us to carry with us," Jake said.

No other explanation was given. He simply turned to Ray and pulled a joint from his cigarette pack. They crouched on the side of the trash bin. I joined them. After passing it between them for awhile, Jake fixed his eyes on me.

"Hit?" was all he said.

I reached for the joint trying to hide my terror. Ray laughed and said, "Everything's gonna be all right 'round here!"

I left for home convinced this job was going to be a piece of cake. None of what my grandfather had told me of his 51 years in the mill registered in my brain as I lay in bed that night. Neither did my father's 40 years of mill experiences. The horror stories they had told around the dinner table about the union, the deaths, the filth and the human degradation were drowned out by the song of freedom that played in my head. I had a job that would pay me enough to make it on my own. My mind was busy putting away the night terrors of poverty, insecurity, welfare, and the abuse of a good-riddance husband. I slept the bliss of the ignorant.

I showed up early the second day too. I found an empty locker and filled it with my bath toiletries and towels. I was ready for the day. I still had about half an hour before work started, so I made my way to the mechanics' shop to buy a Coke. The mill was strangely quiet. I asked a mechanic why there wasn't any noise. He looked at me funny and said, "The mill is down, nobody's out here but us and you laborers."

I paid him for my drink and told him to have a good day.

"You better hope that on yourself," he said and laughed.

That morning I was assigned with Ray, Jake and two other new employees who had hired in a week earlier. I was told that our job was on the end shear scrap incline conveyor. Jake told us to grab a garbage bag and some extra gloves. We strolled down the outside of the mill for about a half mile. Already the day promised to be a hot one. Jake signaled for us to enter the building and the nightmare began.

We picked our way over the roll line to a set of stairs leading underground. Jake stopped on top and smiled. "Now you're about to find out why everyone calls laborers the Mole People," he said as he climbed down the stairs. I fell in line behind the last man.

We continued our downward descent. The light became dimmer and the walls and machinery became dirtier. The black ooze that dripped from the walls and staircases made us all stop and suit up. We tore holes for our heads and arms in the garbage bags and slipped them on. All except Jake. He was so huge, he would have had to split it down the front and wear it like an ill-fitted coat. On the last two floor levels, the quagmire covered every inch in the room. Even the single light bulb dangling over the pit dripped with grease.

When the first man started retching, Jake casually pointed to the far corner.

"What the fuck is that smell?" the man cried.

"Rancid grease," Jake said.

A second man puked down the front of his garbage bag. Jake just shook his head in disgust, then bent down to the task at hand.

The machines were greased continuously to make them run smooth with a combination of axle grease and animal fat, which dripped down to the basement. The heat caused it to go rancid.

Our job was to wrestle pieces of scrap steel weighing between ten and two hundred pounds out of the grease and put them onto a conveyor belt that disappeared somewhere out of our sight. Ray joined in the work next. Within minutes he was puking in the corner with the other men.

As a child, a car accident had taken my sense of taste and smell. What I had always considered a curse was now a blessing. I joined Jake in the knee-high muck. I heaved and pulled on the scrap until I felt the veins on the back of my neck bulge. Jake reached above him and pulled down a crow bar hidden in the blackness. With the help of the bar, the tar-like grease let loose more easily. Jake never tried to help me unless he saw that I was wrestling with a piece that weighed more than I did. Ray composed himself and joined us in the pit with only an occasional dry heave.

At lunch, one of the men asked Moe how come he didn't have to puke.

"I stick ear plugs up my nose," he grinned.

We all made it through our first turn in the mill. As we came out of the pit and into the sunshine, squinting from the dark, Moe laughed out loud and said, "Mole People!"

After washing the grease from my hair for the fourth time, I left for home. I was so tired that I could hardly hold onto the steering wheel of my car. I turned off the radio and heard my father and my grandfather talking in my head. Suddenly, everything they had ever told me about the mills became very important to remember.

Day One

Jennifer Jones

I need a job. For months I've been putting off the inevitable and searching my soul, wondering how I became an unwed mother living at home with her parents and siblings. Where did I go wrong?

I've been paralyzed by fear and uncertainty. I've thought hard about things. It seems I can do one of two things—get a job or go on welfare. But what am I qualified to do? How can I provide for my child?

It doesn't take me long to figure it out. My dad quietly informs me that he is not raising any more children. He doesn't have to say anything else. I will have a job and I will have one quick. I will get a job in the mill.

It's 1970 and almost anyone can get a job in the mill if they want one. It's rumored someone could start at one mill in the morning, quit, and be hired by another mill by the afternoon. My only impression of the mill is a place that is huge and looming, dark and smoky, with an orange sky. I am already in my own black abyss and I don't want to work in a place that looks the way I feel. But none of this matters. I need a job and the mills are hiring.

It takes me about two weeks to get my job at Inland Steel. It's said to be one of the best mills around because they seldom lay off and they treat their employees like family. This, coupled with the fact that a bus runs straight to the mill, makes it an attractive place to work. I don't have a car.

When I apply, the personnel office wants me to wait for a specific position. It takes my calling and calling to convince them how serious I am about needing a job.

Finally, the day is here when I am a full-fledged employee. Part of me is glad for the job, but the biggest part of me is at the lowest point of despair. The only thing that keeps my feet going is the echo I hear in my head of my dad saying he will not raise anymore children. And if he wouldn't, and I couldn't, who would? There is nobody but me. I just want a paycheck that will allow me to take care of my child.

In the new employee orientation there is a group of us sitting in a room watching a movie on the steelmaking process. While the video covers the whole process, I only focus on the furnaces and the open hearths where I can see hot liquid steel being poured. I just know that is where I am going to end up. I can see me now sweating and trying to avoid being killed.

They shake our hands and say, "Welcome aboard." While they make it seem like a good thing, it looks like my worst nightmares are coming true.

They begin to divide us up depending on where we are going to work. I am dropped off at a place called No. 3 Cold Strip. Maybe that means it is going to be cold in there. Maybe I won't have to work in a hot place. But how cold is cold? Our first stop is the department personnel office. We fill out a few more forms and receive a hard hat and goggles. The next stop is the women's locker room. There are about fifty lockers, two showers, and a couple of toilets. So far it doesn't seem too bad. Maybe all of my fears have been for naught, but I still wait for the other shoe to fall. After all, we are in the mill, and I have my own ideas of what a mill is all about.

We go into the Cold Strip mill. We descend about five steps and we turn down a long corridor. The corridor is dimly lit and the walls are painted a pale yellow. As far as the eye can see, yellow covers everything. I can feel my heart start to pound. I can feel my hands start to sweat. I try to remain calm and act nonchalant, but I am sure my darting eyes betray me.

We start walking down the corridor. I hear a low rumble and what sounds like a car horn blowing. I ask myself, *What would a car be doing inside a building?* We keep walking. *Just keep moving. Stay with the guide,* I keep telling myself. We finally reach an opening in the wall of yellow. Now the low rumble is a loud roar. My heart is beating so loud I am sure everyone can hear it. We turn into the opening where we have five steps to climb. My legs are trembling and I'm really afraid but I have to go on. I climb the steps, reach the top of the opening, and my eyes stretch open wide.

How do I begin to describe what I am seeing? How can I describe things I've never seen before? The only thing I know for sure is that there are people everywhere. There are people in overhead cranes. The cranes are like single-seat trolleys on the ceiling and are used to transport coils, scrap, and any other objects that need to be moved from place to place. There are coils rolling on a mill, coils stacked on the floor, and coils on the edge of coil tractors. There are people walking, talking, sweeping, mopping, and just standing still. It is like a three-ring circus. My head keeps spinning so I can catch all the acts going on simultaneously. The noise is incredible, with horns blaring and tractors beeping. I can't even think or even hear the guide talk.

I am wrong about how I thought the mill would look. It isn't black and smoky, nor is it cold inside the Cold Strip building. But this isn't taking away from my fears and dismay of the mill. My guide starts to walk again, and I follow. The building is huge. It appears to be about five football fields in length and width. As we get further into the building, the noise level begins to diminish. I begin to pay more attention to my surroundings and hope that I can let go of some of my fears.

We walk so far down, away from all the hustle and bustle that greeted us when we first came up on the floor, that now it is almost complete silence. It comes as a surprise when I hear a scream. I look at my guide and he does not seem to have heard it, so I think that maybe I hadn't heard it either. Maybe it was just my nerves screaming internally. But no, there it is again—a human scream! The hairs on the back of my neck begin to prickle. I look over at my guide and now I can tell he hears something as well. The sound is coming from the direction we are headed in. While my guide begins to speed up, I want to turn and run the other way. But how can I when this is my first day and I have no idea how to get back? I have been too busy feeling sorry for myself to pay attention to the way we came. There is nothing to do but keep going.

The further we go, the louder the screams are. By now, we are practically running. Is someone injured? Has something fallen on someone? It is obvious by the screams, which are getting louder and louder, that something is terribly wrong. We finally turn the corner and see a woman bent over clutching her chest, screaming while tears are streaming down her face. I don't know what to do. I don't know what to say. There is no blood but she is obviously in pain. I step back while my guide attempts to calm her. He reaches out to touch her and she screams even louder. Every nerve in my being is now on edge. Every thought in my head is screaming, *I told you not to come to the mill! I told you that you don't belong here!* I want to join her in screaming, but I know deep down inside that no matter why she is screaming, no matter what is wrong, I will have to weather the storm because like it or not, I need a job to take care of myself and my son. This is my first day at Inland Steel and I have a job.

Going to the Mill

Gary Novotny

Going to the mill for the first time was similar to going to kindergarten long ago. I didn't want to go. I had feelings of dread. It felt like being separated from my mother, father, and siblings—from the familiar world of childhood. The feeling of resignation was lurking inside like a smiling possum.

I knew what was happening. Going to the mill meant that I had finally lost. It meant giving up the dream of breaking through to some self-actualizing vocation. I had to betray myself so I could go on. It was my duty to provide for my family. Money was something, even if I couldn't be the man from *Father Knows Best*.

But there were other complications. I heard Polonius speak to Laertes: "This above all, to thine own self be true. And as surely as the night follows the day, thou cans't not then be false to any man." Could I ever be part of the world of words and emotions? Of art and nature?

I turned to the mill the same way that a man in deep water clings to a buoy. It was the only thing that could save me and keep me afloat. The job furnished me with the materials to build a vessel for my family. But eventually, it didn't appear seaworthy to them so they got out. I was a cardboard captain. Well, maybe they were as tired as I was. Heavy with it. They say that fatigue makes cowards of us all. Does this include God?

I was late the first day. I overslept. It was very uncharacteristic of me, but full of meaning. I walked in to see the scrubby, rough bodies and faces. Some of them were wearing shiny new hard hats. Some of them had Indiana haircuts underneath. Looking at the faces and bodies, I knew they would be turned into men made of mill dust—lungs coated with rolling oil, sore knees, strained backs, missing fingers, bent necks and vacated intellects. All were people who were previously whole and healthy.

Please! I thought to myself. *Will someone pour water on them and perk them up a bit?* Thirsty houseplants.

Time is warped in the steel mill. It speeds up, slows down or ceases altogether. Standing at my station on the coil annealing line, the drone of machinery and the sound of flying, slicing sheet steel hits my ears. I'm awed by the noise and vibrations all around. The screaming nonsense is all mine now. I'm part of it. I look up. There is no sky, no sun, stars, or planets overhead. The darkness isn't divided from day by the passage of time, but by the halo of illumination around the mill's eyes; lights suspended from the blackness high above. No blue skies, baby! It's a cold, hard smack in the face. I wanted, and still want, to kill the mill. Slay the robotic dragon beast. My hatred for shift work and for what it does is a primal hatred. It places our minds, bodies and souls in jeopardy.

There are times when the dread of leaving for work is palpable. I've noticed it after I've laced up my shoes, grabbed my bag, and I'm standing by the door. I'm just waiting to be sucked out. But it's crazy as hell because there are actually times when I flee to the mill to get away from the other half of my life's journey. Oh Lord, I know I've been forever changed by the conflict between these two lives. Being immersed in the mill, I've become like the steel I work: cold, hard, sharp, heavy, dirty, bent, flawed, and rusting. Yet, through others' eyes, I'm useful, durable, and to an extent, even valuable.

SECTION II: The Way It Was

From An Inferno

Marty Marciniak

Minerals ripped from the dark bowels of the earth were transformed into metal by the unyielding power of fire snatched from the sun. So too were the men who harnessed the heat to melt the ores to become a new element under the light of the law. The 1935 Wagner Act served as a catalyst to give the workers of the mills and the mines a new life as the Steelworkers Organizing Committee in 1936.

With a loan of $500,000 and 150 veteran organizers from John L. Lewis' fledgling Congress of Industrial Organizations, the SWOC grew in influence and strength as its membership exploded from 125,000 in January 1937 to 510,000 by the following May. Fierce resistance to union organizing and outright defiance of the law by employers was no match for the astute leadership of such labor pioneers as Phillip Murray, Van Bittner, Clinton Golden and Harold Ruttenberg. However, it was the courage and the determination of the thousands of shop-floor workers that truly brought the union into the mills unlike ever before.

With the dignity of their work secured by their union cards and contracts, Steelworkers met the challenge of providing the backbone for industrial expansion at home and abroad. When the dark clouds of Fascism spread over Europe, the Steelworkers patriotically accepted the federally imposed wage freezes and offered no-strike pledges "for the duration."

As the SWOC evolved into the United Steelworkers of America in 1942, these men and women of steel were producing countless tons of steel at a record setting pace. From this heaviest of heavy industries, "Liberty Steel" was set afloat as warships and sent aloft as bombers . . . this time to fight a worldwide battle against a different type of oppression.

By the close of the decade, the USWA had grown to 800,000 members, and, along with other CIO unions, was creating the earliest forms of a proud new American middle class.

The Card

Kathi Wellington Dukes

I'm sitting in a union grievance meeting waiting to argue my points. The left side of my head feels like it's been cleaved with an ax. What started as a dull thud this morning has turned into a migraine by afternoon. Problems, problems, problems, and none of them my own. Each raised voice buries the axe a little deeper into my skull. The arguments are going nowhere. The meeting is running late with no end in sight. I wish I could blink and make it all disappear. The problems aren't going away and the solutions are never presented. Maybe I should just accept defeat and crawl home to my warm, dark bedroom for some much-needed sleep.

I shift my weight to my right hip and feel the pinch of The Card in my rear pocket. I reach back and adjust the metal rectangle, the size of a Social Security Card. I run my fingers over the letters etched in its brass face. As the debate drags on, my ears muffle the sharp retorts. The low voice of my grandfather tells me he's not happy with my attitude.

"An injury to one is an injury to all," he whispers.

I close my eyes and visualize his face. The years have blurred the edges. I can barely distinguish his once-sharp, chiseled jaw and piercing gray eyes. With every pulsing throb of my head, he fades in and out; his strong voice rumbling like distant thunder: "Don't half-step your job, Duchess. You were raised better than that. You better fight the good fight til you die."

God knows he did.

The Duke was a steel-working man. For fifty-one years he ate the dirt of the mills, like his father before him and his son afterward. Hired into the open hearth as a child of sixteen, he witnessed the devastation of the Hay Market Massacre, fought in the Wildcat strikes of '29 and '59, and died before cashing his first pension check. He was the original owner of The Card.

The Duke and his brother traveled by boxcar to Indiana from the coal mines of Pennsylvania, looking for a better life than the mines had to offer.

They were both hired by U.S. Steel. My grandfather was the brawn and his older brother was the brain and the mill sorted them out. The brother was sent up the ladder to a job in accounting, The Duke continued to eke out a living by the strength of his back. When his brother went salary and my grandfather went union, the feud began.

Never again to speak to one another, the brothers lived on opposite sides of the same street. As a child, my father got the worst beating of his life for crossing that street on his bike. My grandfather beat him with a belt all the way home. Until then, my father didn't even know he had an uncle, even though it was his only living relative in the country. My father never laid eyes on his uncle until The Duke died.

After the funeral, my father became the owner of The Card. He found it as he sorted through the remains of my grandfather's only belongings. No gold or diamonds, no money or antiques, just some old suits and a box of papers. The Card was nestled at the bottom of the box. My father carried it for the rest of his 43 years in the mill, where he worked as a switchman on the railroad. He swore it gave him strength in the winter when the snot froze in his nose, and in the summer when sweat trickled down the crack of his ass.

He told me The Card had mystical power in the hands of someone who believed in it. The Card got its power from the workers who had fought and died to make the union possible. He said the strongest power was the power of the people. The bosses, management, capitalists, and the government were all afraid of the power the unions held, he said. He gave me The Card when I started my 30-year prison term at the mill. With no sons to pass it on to, he gave it to me saying, "You might not have a pecker, but you've got more balls than most men I've met." He made me promise to carry The Card no matter where my life took me in the mill. It has been a promise I've kept, with pleasure.

The foreman tearing up papers in the front of the room rouses me back to the reality at hand. The meeting is coming apart at the seams. I clear my throat, scan my papers, and walk to the front of the room. I launch into a tirade that lasts a full hour. The footwork and information I had gathered before the meeting pays off. On this day, the brothers and sisters I represent in the union receive the benefit of more than 100 years of Steelworker heritage. When they come to thank me for solving their problems, I can take little credit. It's the mystical power of a simple brass card, issued by I.W. Abel and David J. McDonald to my grandfather for his 50-year honorary membership to the United Steelworkers of America, Local 1066.

Hey Johnny! I Got My SWOC Button!

Marty Marciniak

The old Chevy chugged past the Jefferson Hotel, lurched around the corner onto Third Avenue and parked across from the South Shore track yard. Leon hailed the driver.

"Hey, Mikhal!" he called, "Where's Johnny?"

"Pa's got him working on the chicken coop, so he couldn't come along for the ride this time," Mikhal said. "Hey, you got a lot of laundry there for Ma, huh? You been working good, huh?"

"Pretty good, but I hope Wiktoria can wash up these shirts and pants for me on the sly again," Leon said. "You know how Ma frets about me working in the mills. I don't want her to see no burned-up clothes."

"There ain't nothin' that goes on at the farm that Ma don't know about, Leon," Mikhal said rolling a cigarette. "Never was."

"Hah! Hope you're wrong about that," Leon said. "Let's go."

"So, you been working good?" Mikhal asked. "You got money for Pa? The thresher's broke, and the baler needs parts, too."

"Then let's get goin' if there's that much work to do when we get home."

The ancient roadster limped into the farmyard from the highway and groaned to a halt by the woodshed, sputtering steam and dripping crankcase oil. The dog was barking its fool head off and Leon yelled at it to shut up, but it wouldn't stop. Leon hollered again, this time in Polish and that did the trick. He'd forgotten the dog only understood one language.

Johnny came running across the yard as fast as his bare feet could carry him and he jumped into his big brother's outstretched arms.

"Hey, Johnny!" Leon said. "You get bigger every time I see you, huh? You gonna be big and strong like me someday soon, huh? You gonna be a big strong steelworker, huh?"

"You bet, Leon! I'm gonna be like you! Hey, you got money for Pa?"

"Yeah, yeah, yeah. Leon's got money! Hah! You glad to see me or my money?"

"You, Leon," Johnny said, carrying Leon's laundry bundle back to the house with him. "I'm glad to see you!"

"I know, I know. I'm just making a joke with you, huh? Hey, later we'll talk, huh? I got a secret to tell you. Boy, do I got a story!"

"You bet, Leon!" Johnny said. "You bet!"

Inside the house, Ma complained that Leon looked too skinny and that he probably wasn't eating right. She speculated that his sleeping room probably had bedbugs and that he probably went to too many saloons. Ma was certain that Gary, Indiana was no place for her good Catholic boy, so she questioned him in detail about the churches there and how often he'd been saying his rosary.

After Leon told her what she wanted to hear, she begrudgingly accepted his half-truth evasive answers as the best she was going to get, and she excused Leon to go see his Pa in the barn.

Jesus, Leon thought to himself. *Pa's starting to look old. Every time I come back for a couple of days, he looks older than I think he should. Maybe Ma does too but I just don't see it in her so easy. Or maybe I don't want to.*

"Hello, Papa, how are you? I got money, Papa. Lots of good days in the mill."

He knows, dammit, he knows. The split second when our eyes meet and I have to look away. He knows good an' well there are no "good days" in the mill. Pa and Ma came to America from Poland when Yosef was just a baby and Katrina was only half-grown in Ma's womb. Ma was only, what, fifteen? Sixteen? Only a few years older than Johnny is now. Pa worked the Pennsylvania coal mines and steel mills for a few years, but merciful God! How that must've scared him—and scarred him—scarred his spirit and his soul. Closed up in a mill or mine like that—no wonder he finally packed up everybody and up and went back to Poland saying he'd rather be a peasant farmer under the open sky for the Czar than be a slave holed up in the mills or mines. But then the new Czar came along and they had to come back to America again. Pa's not educated, but he's not stupid. This time they stayed on the trains all the way through Pennsylvania and didn't get off until Whiting, Indiana. They bought this farm near Otis and he worked the farm and factories (again) to get enough to bring over his six younger brothers and their families too. Yeah, Pa KNEW. He knew about "good days in the mill," but he also knew about money. This damn Depression!

"You got a sick horse, Papa? You need medicine?"

"Ach! No medicine! She be better soon."

That evening after supper, Leon sharpened Johnny's stubby pencil with his jackknife and used it to figure out with Ma and Pa how much money they needed to set aside for the church, the bank note, various merchants, and the sock under the mattress.

The next morning, as much as Leon would have loved to sleep in, Johnny and the noisy little ones would have none of it. Two of Pa's brothers, Anton and Stephan, were still without steady work and for the last few years, on and off, some of their kids stayed on the farm for a month or two, sometimes longer. It was toughest on Ma, but Leon's sisters helped out. The older kids could do some of the chores, but they all had to eat. This was a good farm, though. Pa's a good farmer—good with livestock and with the crops. Nobody ate fancy around here, but nobody went hungry either.

"So, what's your secret, Leon? Tell me your story! Ain't you up yet?"

"Whoa, Johnny! Let me get dressed first, huh? You done your chores yet? You tended to the cows? You feed the pigs?"

"All done, Leon. C'mon. I'll tell you a secret too. I'll show you my secret place in the woods to pick the best berries!"

Of course Leon already knew where the best wild berries grew. He was raised on this farm, too, same as Johnny.

Walking through the dewy south pasture, Leon let Johnny lead. They filled a pail with the ripest, marble-sized blackberries and then sat down next to the creek on a log to eat some.

"So, c'mon, Leon, tell me. Tell me your secret."

"Here, Johnny, look at this," Leon said lifting his lapel to reveal a printed steel button the size of a nickel. "I got my SWOC button!"

"What's a *swock?*" Johnny asked, puzzled.

"Look right there, Johnny. See? Steel Workers Organizing Committee. S.W.O.C. I joined the union!"

"So, what's that?"

"It's all us guys in the mill. Well, not all, but most. Not the bosses or the foremen, just us guys. We sticks together, helps each other out. You know, we watch each other's backs."

"I still don't think I understand," Johnny said.

"Well," Leon thought a while. "You remember a couple of years ago when them Swede brothers beat you up, took your spinner top, and called Jania names? You remember what happened?"

Johnny nodded, wide-eyed. "You bet I do!"

"Sure. Me, Yosef, Mikhal and Walter . . . we paid them Swede boys a visit. Was them Swede boys ever mean to you and Jania again?"

"Oh no, Leon. They leave us be. Everybody who seen it leaves us be."

"And you got your spinner top back, right? And they fall all over themselves telling Jania they's sorry, right?"

"Yup."

"Well, it's like that with the union, Johnny. Somebody makes trouble for us, then, by hell, they get trouble back from all of us!"

"You beat people up, Leon? Sister Mary Regina at school says we're not supposed to fight."

"No, it's not like fighting with fists. Well, maybe sometimes . . . but mostly it's fighting with words. We fight with words on paper about what we thinks is right. We got a contract! A contract signed by John L. Lewis himself!" Leon's chest swelled noticeably.

"Wow!" Johnny said, wondering who John L. Lewis was. "Who makes trouble for you in the mill, Leon?"

"Ah," Leon said, sweeping his arm through the air. "Them bastard foremens, mostly. Telling us guys what we gotta do. Even when it ain't right, we gotta do it."

"Like when Sister says I gotta learn my ciphers at school, but I don't wanna?"

"Well, not exactly. Father Henry says the sisters are doing God's work, an' I guess that's the truth. But these goddamn bastard foremens in the mill, they act like they are gods, but they ain't!"

Leon punctuated his words with a clenched fist slapping into his open palm. Johnny liked it when Leon used swear words. It somehow made him feel more grown-up, closer to Leon. Leon trusted him not to snitch to Ma. But it scared him too, though. It was a sign that Leon was getting mad about something and meant business. Johnny remembered that Leon cussed them Swede boys a blue streak.

"So what else about the union, Leon? Tell me more."

"Well, I been to some meetings. Big ones with lots of us from the mill. I heard speeches from regular guys like me, and some from union men from Pittsburgh or Chicago or places like that. Sometimes they use big words that I don't understand, but I listen anyways an' I learn an' I figure out."

Leon paused. "Some guys in the mill who don't like the union, Johnny, they say the big-word, fancy-talk fellas is agitators or socialists or Bolsheviks. Johnny, I don't know 'bout that, but, damn it, I know working in the mill. An' I know what's right. An' what they says is right!

"And you know what else, Johnny?" Leon said. "I found out that the things that I think ain't right, well, lotsa other guys in the mills think the same thing! Hell! We ain't asking for much. We just want what's fair! By the rules; no cheating. You know, like the rules in checkers or mumbly-peg or some other game. That's what the contract is, I guess—the rules about what's fair, or at least what's closer to fair than no rules at all. And if we got a contract writ down, y'see, nobody can cheat later by making up the rules as we go."

"Leon?"

"Yeah, Johnny?"

"Who's that fella you said with my name? John . . ."

"John L. Lewis, he's the President." Leon says.

"I thought Mr. Roosevelt was the President."

Leon's eyes twinkled as he set his hand on Johnny's shoulder.

"You're right, Johnny, he is. But John L. Lewis is the President of the CIO, the Congress of Industrial Organizations. See right here on my button? C.I.O. That's like a union of a lot of unions. Just like Mr. Roosevelt is the President of the U.S.A., John L. Lewis is the President of the CIO—of all the unions. Well, most of the best ones anyways."

"We heard Mr. Roosevelt on the radio at church once," Johnny said. "I wish we had a radio."

"For a radio you need 'lectricity," Leon said grinning. "An' ain't no farms around here got no 'lectricity."

"Well, lemme see that button again, Leon" Johnny said, fidgeting with excitement. "Dues paid? What does that mean?"

"That means I paid my money to belong," Leon said with an almost imperceptible nod. "And, warn't no dues steward hafta chase me down for it neither. I signed my card an' paid my dues in cash money and got my button right there at the meeting in front of everybody. I don't care who knows I'm with the SWOC. It feels real good to me, 'cause I don't gotta be afraid of nothing or nobody no more. It's like the taxes Pa pays on the farm, Johnny. Pa pays tax to own this piece of land an' he don't really mind it, no matter what he says, 'cause it's his land. I pays my union dues an' I'm glad to, 'cause now I got my own piece of the union. This button to me is like the tax receipts Pa keeps tucked under the Bible. I figure it's a real bargain to be part of something as big an' as right as the union for only a few bucks in dues."

"I heard Ma tellin' Pa last night about seein' the same burns on your arms when you washin' up for supper that Pa used to have when he worked in the mills," Johnny said. " Did Pa used to be in the union, too?"

By God, Mikhal was right, Leon thought. *Ma really does know everything.*

"Unions was different then. Pa couldn't join them unions," Leon said. "An' the laws was different then, too. That counts for a lot."

"Can I have this button, Leon? Please? Please?"

A softness glowed in Leon's eyes that he reserved only for Johnny.

"Oh, no, Johnny. I'm really sorry, but I need it for the dues inspections they sometimes got at the gates. A fine thing for me to get caught without my SWOC button! My buddies would never let me live that down. I'm sorry, Johnny, but more than that, I *need* this button. This button helps me feel connected up to somethin' big, somethin' important, somethin' for my future and maybe someday, yours too. But I tell you what, Johnny, I'll bring you one when I get another the next month when I pay. OK, Johnny? Will that be OK? That's the best I can do for now."

"OK, Leon, sure . . . you bet."

Johnny was disappointed but he knew he'd get a SWOC button someday. A promise from Leon was as good as gold.

"Hey, Johnny, we gotta get back. I gotta fix that damned old thresher today. You gonna help me?"

"You bet, Leon. You bet!"

True to his word, Leon eventually brought Johnny his SWOC buttons— a whole handful after awhile (just like he brought laundry home for Ma). Johnny kept the SWOC buttons in a sock under his mattress. He'd sometimes lie awake and think about Leon and the things he said. He tried to imagine the mills and the union meetings and such, although he couldn't really. But he *knew*—he knew that if all that lit such a fire under Leon, then by hell it was what he wanted for himself too. He knew that he wanted to follow Leon into the mills and the union . . . maybe even work with him and sit next to him at the union meetings and have his own SWOC button every month. Johnny knew all of this in a way that only a 12-year-old boy can know about what a big brother tells him, and for Johnny it was as true as it could possibly be.

But time passes, things change. As fate would have it, Johnny got drafted right off the farm into World War II when he reached his eighteenth birthday. He didn't go into the mills until after he returned from overseas. He was lucky. One of Uncle Stefan's sons died there. But when Johnny finally mustered out of the Army and into the mills, there was no more SWOC. By then it was the USWA, the United Steelworkers of America.

Leon moved to Detroit and built Fords with the UAW until he retired and died a month later. And Johnny—like a lot of people who grew up in the Depression—tried not to think too much about those days. The war overshadowed those memories of the farm anyway. Johnny never thought about the SWOC button again.

Not until a day that came after much time had passed and many things had changed. It wasn't until long after Johnny had a son who followed him into the mills, like Leon and Johnny had followed Pa. And not until Johnny's son came to know about some things like his dad and old Uncle Leon must have known once, too. But sometimes knowledge is just more important and just becomes more valuable only through self-discovery (even if it's about nothing more important than where the best wild berries grow). Then it matters more. Then it means something.

That's why it's important to look back at yesterday to help figure out today, because tomorrow, that knowledge will mean something. Maybe to you, maybe to someone else, but it will matter.

Jania, now known as Aunt Jane, had also learned long ago how to retain knowledge. She noticed that Johnny's son sometimes waved his arms or set his jaw exactly like Leon, and later Johnny, used to do. She noticed that even casual small talk about work or "what's right," or "what's fair" at family gatherings lit the same kind of fire in him she'd seen before in her brothers many years ago. She'd learned from Ma how to always know about what goes on—so she knew about that old SWOC button. And on that day, it only took her a few minutes to go to that old four-quart mason jar of buttons, safety pins, and whatnot from the farm, and dump it out on the bedspread. And there it was . . . the only one left. She put it in Johnny's son's hand and said, "This belonged to your Uncle Leon. I want you to have it now. Go show it to your dad."

He sat down beside Old John, as Johnny had come to be known, and said, "Look, Dad. Look at what Aunt Jane gave me."

Yes, time passes; and yes, some things surely do change. But some other things just as certainly never change—or perhaps they only change back again. Old John held the button. His eyes studied it carefully and then he clenched it tight in his fist for a long while. He seemed to be remembering things he'd never really forgotten—more so a process of mentally reviewing some series of events that brought him to where he was today, right here, right now. It was a set of links in a chain that stretched back to before he was even born—back to Pennsylvania coal fields and mill towns and beyond. The links extended forward as well, to and through the younger man who sat beside him. And Old John noticed without surprise that almost every link had a bit of Leon's mettle cast into it with alloys of respect and admiration; with elements of guidance and example.

Old John looked at the button again. It was a relic from his past, but it was also a catalyst for a long overdue conversation that was about to take place, right here, right now. And there was no doubt in his mind that it would, from this day forward, become a touchstone, a guidepost, a talisman, that would forge future chain links as time would pass . . . as things would change.

Old John gently placed the button back in his son's hand and said, 'Hey, son, I want to tell you about when your old Uncle Leon said to me: "Hey, Johnny! I got my SWOC button!"'

Company Town
Sandy Dunn

I grew up in the town of Sparrows Point, Maryland, which was right outside the gates of Bethlehem Steel's blast furnaces. The oaks and maples that lined the streets were so old that their branches formed a solid canopy over the passing cars. Light would filter onto the street in patches. If I close my eyes, I can see my friends playing in streets that were dusted red from open hearths that were practically in our back yard.

The Red Rocket trolley ran down the middle of Main Street. As a treat on Fridays, my mother and I would take the Red Rocket into Highland Town in Baltimore to shop after school. The trolley never turned around. It just went back and forth. The seats would flip so you could face the front, depending on which direction the trolley was headed. The conductor would switch ends of the trolley at the end of the line. It felt like we were traveling faster than the wind when we glided across the bridge which connected Sparrows Point to a little town called Dundalk. I would open my window to feel the wind of the Back River on my face. I would close my eyes and dream I was on a voyage somewhere across the ocean like England or France.

As kids we never took notice of the red dirt everywhere or questioned the quality of the air we breathed. We never thought about it. We were just happy our families had good jobs and a nice place to live. All we knew was that the steel business was booming and everyone was making money. No one locked their doors at night. It was thought that one skeleton key fit all the doors in town anyway. Besides, everyone knew each other.

Bethlehem Steel owned the entire town and employees were encouraged to rent houses from the company. Bethlehem Steel took care of all repairs on your house: plumbing, electrical—you name it, their employees fixed it. Bethlehem Steel also painted all the houses inside and out every two years. The only problem was that the only color combinations were green and gray, or brown and gray.

The houses were row homes and the amount of rent depended on whether you had indoor or outdoor plumbing. We had outdoor plumbing which suited us just fine. I remember once when my Uncle Tim was visiting us and he went outside to use the bathroom. The toilets flushed automatically as soon as you got off the toilet seat. He turned around just as it was flushing and was so startled that his false teeth fell out of his mouth. The water carried them away before he knew what had happened. Man, did he get mad! He was careful in the bathroom after that.

The basements were carved from stone because the homes were built on solid rock. I loved to play down there. We had an ancient coal-burning furnace that sat in the corner. It looked like an iron monster with eyes and a grill for teeth. The walls would sparkle like diamonds when the fire burned. It was both scary and exciting. I remember my father putting a big fish that he had caught near Pennwood Wharf onto a long paddle and sticking it directly into the furnace. It was delicious.

We had backyards and front yards with grass and flowers the same as anyone else. It was a pretty town; not as ugly as some would think. Most of the women were housewives. They did the same things other housewives did, but laundry posed a special problem for the women of Sparrows Point. They had to check the wind before they hung it out to dry. If it was blowing from the direction of the furnaces, they didn't put their clothes on the line because they'd be covered in red dust by the end of the day. This didn't bother them though. It was just their way of life; part of the natural order of things, like rainfall or snow. Most of the women grew up there themselves.

Generations lived, worked and died in Sparrows Point. My father was a foreman at the steam department. His father lived and worked in Sparrows Point before him. My mother remembers that children would take lunch pails right into the mills to deliver them to their fathers. No safety hats or anything. This changed by the time I was a child.

My father was only two minutes from home, so he came home for lunch every day. When he came home, my mom had dinner ready for him at exactly 4 p.m. She would dress up and wait by the door for him to come home. My parents were very close and definitely creatures of habit. You could set a clock by them.

I remember lying on my sister's bed at night and looking out the window at the blast furnaces. I could see the tall, beautiful blue flame leaping into the air from the blast furnace. I lay there for hours, mesmerized.

Sparrows Point was self-contained. You never had to leave it if you didn't want to. Everything you needed was right outside your door. My mom would give me money and I would walk to the Phone Company to pay the phone bill. I can still remember my phone number:183R. The operators worked so fast. It fascinated me. They wore headsets and pushed plugs into holes that would light up, asking, "Number please." We had party lines that we shared with other families. I liked to pick up the phone and eavesdrop on my neighbors' conversations. I knew as much about their family as I did about my own.

We never worried about being robbed. That kind of thing never happened in Sparrows Point. We had our own Police Department, also owned by the company. The town consisted of homes, banks, five churches (each representing a different denomination), grocery stores, and a very large drug store. The movie theater had a bowling alley in the basement. I went to school with the young boys who worked there resetting the pins.

The only thing that you couldn't buy in town was alcohol. No bars were allowed. You had to leave town if you wanted to get drunk.

Bethlehem Steel owned all the schools too. Sometimes I wonder what kind of input the company had in our education.

Mrs. Stern, the principal, ruled with an iron fist. She was a big woman who wore her dark hair pulled back in a bun. She wore glasses and long black dresses that hung loosely to the middle of her shins. Everyone was terrified of her.

Once I was running back to class after a recess on a cold snowy day in January. I saw Mrs. Stern coming my way and I swallowed the piece of gum I was chewing. It made me kind of sick, but it was better than getting caught. If she caught you chewing gum, she forced you to wear it on the end of your nose for the rest of the day. Then she would send a note home to your mother.

The blacks were segregated from the whites and had their own school. It was the late 1940s and early 1950s and no one thought anything of it at the time. That was how people lived back then. I don't know for sure, but I don't believe the black people thought it bad either. It was our way of life.

The man down the street owned a great dog named Barney. He was big, with small whites spots on his nose and a shiny black coat. His big brown eyes always looked so sad. But his tail was always wagging.

His owner would send him to the grocery store with saddlebags on his back and a note in the bag. The ragged old man who worked at the grocery would fill the order form and pack the groceries, including meat, in the saddle bags. Then Barney would walk home—slowly so as not to lose anything—without touching the food. My friends and I would follow him home to see if he could make it without eating something. He never disappointed us.

There were hucksters roaming the streets in horse-drawn carts and trucks. They would ride up and down the streets yelling out what they had for sale. I remember a man named Dennis who sold anything from clothing to flour out of the back of his truck. The variety of items he stocked amazed me. He always carried a big block of cheese and cut off pieces all day for the people buying it. It was covered with dirty fingerprints. It wasn't easy to keep anything clean outdoors in Sparrows Point.

Bethlehem Steel also had a boarding house in town for all the bachelors who worked at the mill. Mr. Bob ran the boarding house. I used to visit him sometimes when he was working outside on a project. He had been seriously injured in an accident in the plate mill.

Mr. Bob was short, skinny and bent. He never told me why his body was stuck that way. But he had other stories to share, most of which involved mill accidents and the crazy things he had witnessed in the mill. We would drink lemonade and relax in the shade for hours until my sister would come to tell me to come home for dinner.

My father was a member of the volunteer fire department at Sparrows Point. When the horn sounded, he dropped everything and ran to the fire. We had a book on our coffee table that listed all of the areas of the mill and town, which corresponded to the number of blows the horn made. Most of my friends' fathers were volunteer firefighters and when there was a fire, the men dashed to the fire station and the wives, wearing their aprons, came out their front doors to talk about where the fire was and what was going on.

The company drugstore was a huge building. I don't think it was originally built to be a drugstore, because it was the biggest drugstore I've seen to this day. You had to climb a tall set of cement steps. It was my favorite place in town and a popular hangout for the cool kids.

Inside, there was a soda fountain where you could get a cherry Coke for a nickel, and an ice cream float for thirty-five cents. They had "penny candy" which was really a penny back in those days. I would walk or ride my bike to the drugstore every day with my friends to buy some candy with change left over from my lunch money. If I had enough change, I would get my favorite—a cherry Coke.

Next door was the local greasy spoon. The bachelors living at the boarding house were usually the only customers. It was called a greasy spoon for a good reason. Everyone else was at home with their families, eating dinner. This was a family town.

We had a newspaper delivery boy who was born with a stump for a right arm. His real name was Lou, but every time he came to the door to collect money, my mom would call out, "Wally, the one-armed paper boy is here." I can still hear her today. It's funny, the little things from your childhood that seem to stay with you forever.

Just about everyone who worked at the mill—from the general manager to the mill laborers—lived in the town. It was built around the turn of the century and many generations lived, worked and died there.

But Bethlehem Steel finally got tired of keeping up with the houses and wanted to build a new blast furnace where the town stood. In 1956, they told us to get out—as if we were unwanted relatives who had come to visit. The company told us we had to move out and they didn't care where.

Families were desperate to find a nice place to live. My family was given an extension and we didn't move out until August. I watched, heartbroken, as my friends moved out of their homes. The company was right behind them with a wrecking ball, smashing houses down. It was frightening, like living in a war zone.

The residents scattered over a few counties when they moved. I lost track of most of my friends. My family moved to Edgemere and our life was never the same. Our fathers still worked at the mill but our sense of community had been shattered. Our new place to live wasn't bad. But it wasn't home.

The only saving grace is that some of my childhood friends work at the plant with me today and I can see them once in a while.

The town of Sparrows Point isn't there anymore. But it will always be the magical place I call home.

SECTION III: Workers We Knew

Hawkeye

Joe E. Gutierrez

Everybody called him Hawkeye.

He was the blackest, the ugliest, and could be the meanest "colored" you ever met in your life. He bragged how every payday he would buy a steak, then bury it somewhere in his back yard for his dog to dig up. He said if he had to work to buy the food, that bitch would have to work to get it.

He didn't want to be called "Negro," "black," "Afro-American," or whatever new name "they" came up with. He never did explain who "they" were, and nobody bothered to ask. He said he was "colored" and that's all there was to it. Nobody argued with him, black or white. We called him anything he wanted to be called.

His birth name was James "Jimmy" Hawkinson. He was born on and grew up on a farm in Mississippi. He said he killed a man when he was sixteen years old. I believed him. Told me that he hated that old white motherfucker, because every night, as soon as he closed his eyes, he could see that son of a bitch's face, laughing. Jimmy said that was one of the reasons he drank. He wasn't sorry he killed him. He was just sorry he couldn't get him off his mind. When I asked him what happened, he just looked away. Never did tell me, and I never asked him again.

He said when he left Mississippi, he never looked back. Didn't even get a chance to say goodbye to his grandma, who raised him. That's the first time I saw the Hawkeye cry. The second time was when his son got killed in a car accident. I was standing next to him by No. 2 line pot, when Hank Durbin, the general foreman, gave him the bad news. Hawkeye was ugly, but he got uglier when he cried. It was only for a second, but he did cry. I turned my head and pretended that I didn't notice, but my heart went out to him. I wanted to cry with him, but I just said I was sorry and walked away. Left him with his pain. He shrugged it off and walked out of the mill. Hawkeye stayed drunk for a month.

But Jimmy could laugh too, and when he laughed, he laughed with his whole soul. His voice was deep and melodious. He could talk with a Bronx accent as well as he could a Mississippi drawl. Spoke some Spanish too.

I always wondered what Jimmy could have been. What he was, though, among other things, was a bookmaker. The Hawk booked numbers for the "Chinaman," a Japanese gangster out of Cicero who was the moneyman for the syndicate. They shot him in the head a few years back. He survived and became an informer for the government. I guess everyone has a breaking point, but I don't think I would turn over for the feds. Just couldn't do it.

Everybody played the numbers. Even the white guys. It was everybody's dream to hit the big one and get out of the mill. Hawkeye would take any bet—nickel, dime—he didn't care. If your number came in, you got paid. He got 10 percent, but that was all right.

Hawkeye was short, stocky and had an immense barrel belly. His head was big and he had small pig eyes. The tip of his nose and the top half of his left ear were missing. He was bowlegged and not a pretty sight to behold. If friendships were based only on looks, Hawkeye would have been friendless. At sixty-three, he was still tough and would kick ass in a minute. He told me that after "it" happened, he hitched a ride to New York City and worked on the docks. He said that's where he grew up, and he meant really *grew up*.

Jimmy had so many scars on his face, you couldn't tell where one ended and the other began. He said those dagos tap-danced on his face with switch blades when they caught him feeling up a white broad. And she was ugly too. He said he never did figure that one out. Nobody wanted her, but they sure as hell didn't want him to have her. Said all he wanted was a taste.

"You know what, Little Joe, I can still see that broad's face," he said. "When they started cuttin' on me, she started screaming, 'Leave him alone!' Then they started cuttin' on her. I didn't remember anything after that, and I didn't feel nothin' either, until later. Never did see her again. Always wondered what happened to her. People come in your life, say a few words that mean something and then they're gone like they never been there. Crazy."

When Hawkeye woke up, he heard someone say, "Man, we got one ugly nigger here! I don't think he's breathing. Looks like he's dead."

When he heard what that man said, he remembered those stories he heard when he was a kid about people being buried alive. Hawkeye said he let out a shout that came up from the bottom of his soul: "I'm alive, motherfucker! I'm alive!"

A month later, he was in Chicago.

When he hired in at Inland, they threw him in the Galvanize Department. Mostly blacks, Mexicans and Puerto Ricans worked there. At the time, it was one of the worst departments in the mill. Hawkeye didn't care. Said he found a home. The Galvanize was bad. Most everybody carried a bottle just to make it through the day. You could hardly see through the smoke and sulfuric acid fumes. The man in the crane caught it all: smoke, acid, everything. The man on the floor had to use a flash light to direct the craneman. Before the modern lines came in, they hand-dipped hot strips of steel into batches of molten zinc. It took two workers with tongs. One on each side of the strip. It was hot and dangerous. Hawkeye loved it.

When they built the new line, Galvanize became the place to work. That's when the company brought the white guys in to run the line. And that's when the Hawkeyes and the Sanchezes and the Villarreals started to raise hell. And that's when the union started to be a union. And if it wasn't for that same union, the company suck-asses would have kept those jobs.

Before Hawkeye retired, he finally became a galvanizing line operator, the highest paying job in the department. Jimmy was a good operator. He knew the job and he could smell when something was wrong. He was a bitch to work with, but other than that, it was OK.

The last time I saw Hawkeye was downtown Hammond, Indiana. I was crossing Hohman Avenue by the old Goldblatts building with my mother. When Jimmy saw me, he swaggered up to us and put out his hand. He was wearing a white suit and a white fedora. He looked like a man who wanted to look like a preacher.

I said, "Mom, this is Jimmy Hawkinson."

Hawkeye took my mother's hand, removed his hat, bowed and said, "Ma'am, I am extremely pleased to meet you. You have a wonderful son, and they call me Hawkeye."

My mother smiled and said, "Thank you." She told me later that Hawkeye was a real gentleman.

I heard they found him dead in his van. He was on his way to Florida. He must have pulled off to the side of the road and fallen asleep. Never woke up. He was only retired for six weeks.

Scottie

Jerry Ernest

An old swing set stands in the yard. It has turned gray and the wood is splitting. You'll get a splinter if you aren't careful. I remember a time when it was new and green. The pressure-treated lumber was still wet. The saw would bind up when we tried to cut through it, Scottie and me.

I met Scott in one of the labor pools in the mid-70s. I started getting laid off and recalled pretty regularly back then. He was tall and thin, almost anorexic. His face was drawn and he had a mousy sort of look about him. His sunken eyes were so blue they sparkled. After I started talking to him, we realized we knew a lot of the same people.

Shift work, poor working conditions, alcohol and drugs took a toll on many relationships in the mill. Scott was no different. He had been through two marriages in a short time.

Our paths crossed many times over the years. Once, after being recalled and working as a laborer at the powerhouse, I saw a Bobcat coming out of the dust. Its lights were on and the horn was blaring.

"Hey, Jerry! Hey, Jerry!" Someone was yelling. It was Scott with a respirator hanging off his neck, his face covered in dirt.

We talked about how the hell we were ever going to get out of this shit hole.

A while later, I saw a job posting hanging onto a board by a single thumbtack. "CARPENTERS NEEDED." A craft job at last! I got a hold of Scott and showed him the posting. He shrugged it off and said he didn't know anything about carpentry. But I was confident we could pass the mill test to become carpenters. I had met some carpenters, while serving an apprenticeship as a blacksmith, and during a layoff in the 80s, I had an opportunity to work in a cabinet shop as a carpenter's helper doing rehab work. I talked him into signing up and we started studying together. Sure enough, we both passed. Scottie aced the test and I passed by the skin of my teeth.

We started working together on a regular basis. For a while, we would follow the lead of other men. He and I were the helpers, but we were craft.

Scott had a sweet tooth. Once, at a restaurant, I ordered a strawberry pie. He had never tried one, but when he did, he was hooked. Life was good.

Working with Scott, I began to see he had some demons. I knew he liked to smoke "flakes"—parsley flakes laced with PCP—but I found out later he liked crack, too. His eyes were always red and vacant. I tried to look out for him; get him to sit down so he wouldn't get hurt. I started getting on his ass too. A lot of us did. I needed to depend on him; the work we do is dangerous. It's our job to make it safe for other people first. Scott started missing time from work and feeling bad all the time. He said he was having trouble with his woman at home.

He finally sought help for his problems. He came back into the gang about a month later. Scott was focused. He started ram-rodding the jobs and I had to fight with him to try and get the lead. He was really trying to help himself.

What bothers me was the treatment Scott got from other workers. Why do guys always rag on a man when he's trying to do the right thing? They tempt him into falling again so they can tell him he's worthless and make themselves feel superior. Like a pack of crazed dogs they descended on him. I got tired of those jerks taunting Scott.

"Hey, Scott, we got the good ones," they would say. "Want some? Come on, you know you do."

It was endless.

"Leave him alone, you ASSHOLES," I screamed at them finally. "You live in a crystal palace that could come down around your ears at any time! FUCK WITH ME! COME ON! COME ON DAMMIT!"

I wanted to rip 'em apart. Scott touched my shoulder and told me it was OK; it didn't bother him. I wish I'd felt that way, because I wanted a piece of their ass.

We worked together regularly for the next year. He bought a Blazer, went through a couple of girlfriends, and started working on his house. He came over to my house and helped me put together the swing set for my girls.

The last time I saw him was a blustery day in March. He and I worked over at the BOF that day. We were covered in dirt. At lunch we got a bite to eat. Scott ordered a strawberry pie.

We had just gotten back to the locker room, showered and changed when the boss came in late and asked me to work over.

"Hell no," I said. "Why didn't you ask me sooner?"

Scott took the assignment. It was in the 56 pickler. I left for home and didn't even say be careful. Scott was scheduled to work with two older men that night. One was getting ready to retire. The other was a shop man. Both good carpenters. Scott, wanting to prove himself, took the lead.

The pickler was a dimly lit, dirty, stinking place. It had that smell in the air—acid. I always hated being there. It felt like you were taking in death with every breath.

Scott knew the dangers. Taking the lead, he walked over the tank and started stripping off the top boards when one of them snapped. Scott fell backwards, disappearing into the hole. The tank had been cooling down. It was 160 degrees and only knee-deep. His fellow crew members rushed to him and held out their arms to pull him out.

His head was down and when he looked up he had tears in his eyes and said, "I'm a dead man. I swallowed this shit."

"Give me your hand!" they screamed.

Scott looked up a second time standing in the knee-deep acid, crying. "I'm dying! I'm dying!" he sobbed.

They finally pulled him out and stripped his clothes off. Someone called for help while others started hosing him down with water. His skin fell off like jelly.

The phone rang that night and my boss told me about the accident. He thought I should know because I was the shop steward.

"There isn't anything you can do," he said. "I just wanted you to know."

I said a prayer and hoped it wouldn't be real bad.

The locker room was still that morning. You could hear some of the men talking as if they were in church. I went looking for the two men who had worked with Scott. The look in their eyes told the story. They looked as if they hadn't been to bed all night. Their eyes were red and puffy and they didn't really want to talk about it. They had to tell that story over and over again, and they were sure the safety people would want the details. You could see the pain in the faces of both men. I was sure they felt the same guilt I was feeling.

I was asked if I would go over to the accident scene. When I got there, I saw Scott's clothes scattered on the floor. I picked them up with rubber gloves. The leather on his shoes had turned white overnight, and I placed them in a bag. I walked up to the tank and peered down into it, the smell of acid was stronger than I ever remembered it.

The acid-soaked boards that had put my friend in the tank were staring me in the face. I never felt so sick in my life. My heart broke because I realized the true horror my co-workers had experienced. I broke down. I didn't do much the rest of the day; just kind of roamed around thinking of how things could have been different if I had just worked over.

They kept Scott doped up and comfortable. He died two days later. All the men had to report to the shop. The company had hired a trauma counselor who wanted to help us deal with our grief. He was talking to all of us, but I couldn't hear him. My thoughts were with my friends. We were strong men who had stuck together many times in the past. I watched as we split up to wander off and let our hearts bleed. Some of these proud men hugged each other and cried.

If I had just worked over. It runs through my mind. Or if I hadn't shown Scott that posting, where would he be today? My God, why? It isn't fair. He had so much to live for. His children lost their dad. I had never met them, but he had talked often about his son and little girl.

We all went to the funeral parlor. His loved ones were there: his mother, the ex-wives, friends, his children, and even the President of the company.

Scottie's little girl couldn't have been older than five. Her blond hair flowed as she played in the room running around and telling people, "Daddy's sleeping." Looking around the room, I saw pain on many of the faces. I had a hard time being there because of the pain and guilt I was feeling. Scottie's little girl came over to me and looked up at me with those bright blue eyes—the same eyes as Scottie—and she said, "Daddy's sleeping."

Thunderbird

Chuck Canty

When I hired at Inland Steel, Antonio Vargas had 25 years in the mill and we were often assigned to work together. Everyone called him Tony or Thunderbird. He got that nickname because he liked to drink cheap wine.

We talked a lot while we worked. He told me that he had lived in Brownsville, Texas as a boy. He said he used to be a brick layer until he moved to East Chicago and got a job at Inland Steel. He tried to get into the mason and brick-layering department when he first hired in, but back then it was an all-white department and they sent him to be a truck mechanic.

I had worked with Tony for about 10 years when he decided to retire at 65. He had over thirty-five years seniority. On his last day, he went to the personnel department to get his retirement papers. The personnel department is where every Steelworker's career begins and ends. The day you hire in at Inland, you go through an induction process that's similar to joining the military or serving the first day of a life sentence in prison. First you fill out a load of paperwork, then you go to the clinic for a complete physical. Then you're photographed and fingerprinted. After a final screening, they tell you when and where to show up for your first day on the job.

That morning, Tony came back to the garage with his papers from personnel and a pass to get his tools out of the plant. I was working on a truck right next to the office when Tony came out. He called me over.

"Hey, Canty, take a look at this," he said, in a low, raspy voice.

He took a picture out of an envelope he was holding and handed me a picture that was taken the day he hired in. I saw the face of a young man with fire in his eyes. I looked back at Tony. He was all wrinkles and gray hair. The fire was gone. A man spends his entire life in a mill and on his last day they just hand him his walking papers. It's like serving a 30-year jail sentence and getting out on parole. No salutes, no badges of honor, no fanfare. Just papers and an old photograph.

"I was a real ladies' man back then," he said. "I had all the women wanting to go with me."

"I'm sure you were," I said.

Just then a foreman walked by. Tony told him he had completed his paperwork and asked him if he could get a ride to the gate. The foreman told Tony he was busy and that he would have to wait.

I felt like laying a pipe over the foreman's head. This was Tony's last day on the job and that dirty, rotten motherfucker treated him with absolutely no dignity or respect.

Tony paced back and forth by the doorway for a few minutes. I looked out the door and saw half a dozen pickups sitting there.

"Come on," I said to Tony. "I'll take you to the gate. Fuck that guy."

We loaded up his tool box and his personal belongings and headed out to the parking lot. I asked Tony why he didn't tell that fat-ass to go to hell, or to go screw himself. Tony said he didn't want to cause a scene on his last day or do anything that would jeopardize his retirement.

We drove to the gates and talked about Tony's plans. Thunderbird was now free to fly. He said he was going to soar out of this stinking mill and never look back. I felt as if I was driving a triumphant Caesar through the streets of Rome.

I dropped him off. We shook hands.

"Take care of yourself," I told him. "And take lots of Inland's retirement money."

I watched him drive away. We may leave here old and broken, I thought to myself, but our spirits can never be crushed.

Wild Bill

Stan Daniloski

Nature's plan is to live in harmony. It has checks and balances built into its program, but once in a while some amoeba runs amok, and the results are usually detrimental to something else in the chain. Kelso was a guy who had an amoeba problem. He was programmed to make life as miserable as possible for everyone around him. He was a mean-natured dude, and there I was nose to nose and toe to toe with that devil. Well, not quite nose to nose; he was a good four inches taller, but I was itchin' to drive that damn hard hat down over his ears.

His name was Bill Kelso, but everybody called him "Wild Bill," a name he really tried to live up to. He had broken company service, and the scuttlebutt was he had been in jail. He was a mean, cantankerous old goat, and at that moment I hated him. His face had more lines than a city map. Fifty-eight years never looked uglier, but he was lean and deceptively strong.

What was I doin'? I had to be crazy to confront Wild Bill. If he didn't kill me, at the least, I'd be fired.

Kelso's sole role in life was to make things as uncomfortable as possible for every junior man in our department. He constantly needled and antagonized all the young helpers and apprentices with his "good ol' boy" meanness and West Virginia spiced cussin'. Some of the men claimed the only reason Kelso held onto his job was because he "had something" on Whitey, our foreman. Maybe he did. Bill used to be a "pusher" for Whitey on a lot of big jobs.

One of Kelso's favorite stunts was to take a new hire to the old sintering plant. The inside of this building had conveyor lines carrying iron ore dust to furnaces that melted the dust into globs of iron to be used in the blast furnaces. On the best of days you could just make out an overhead light through the dust hanging in the air. Kelso would tell his victim to wait right there and not move. Then he went outside and slammed the door shut. Red dirt would come down off the rafters like a waterfall. All the poor sucker could do was wait for the dust to settle so he could find his way out.

Another time, Wild Bill locked a cat in Tom Sweeney's work trailer over the weekend. When Tom opened the trailer on Monday morning, he was knocked down by a wild, half-crazy, starving cat. On still another occasion, he dumped a five-gallon bucket of yellow wire-pulling lubricant on the head of a young helper who crossed his path.

Well, it had to happen sooner or later. One day ol' Bill got me in his sights. He found out that I was Polish, and things went downhill very quickly. He began battering me with Polish "jokes" which were just then becoming "popular" with a certain segment of the population. This disintegrated into name-calling. Square-head and Polack were his favorites. I avoided him at every turn, and tried to let the hurts roll off my back. He knew it bothered me, so he kept up the assault for months.

Kelso and I happened to be on the same job one day. During our lunch break he really worked me over verbally. I went back to work a little early just to get away from him. As I was walking away I heard a lot of laughing. I turned around to see Wild Bill mimicking my walk. "Hey, Polack," he hollered, "is this how a Polack walks?" More laughing.

Bingo! He pushed the right button!

My blood boiled. I grabbed a convenient scrap piece of conduit and started dancin' with the devil. He cursed me and threatened to turn me in to the foreman. I didn't care. I must have looked like a wild man. I thought I saw a flash of uncertainty on his mug. After more cussin' and belly bumpin', Wild Bill turned around, picked up his lunch bucket and went home!

I felt cheated. How could he do this? I desperately wanted to see how that monster looked with his helmet wedged down over his eyes.

The rest of the workday was anticlimactic. When I got home that evening, I felt utterly drained physically. I didn't sleep well that night, and I was up before the alarm went off. I dreaded the day. Then I realized it was Saturday, and I was off for the weekend. Thank God for these little islands of rest during the week.

Monday did show in its turn, and I was back in line punching in with the rest of the gang. Wild Bill clocked in and walked past me without a word. On the job he ignored me. I was uncomfortable. I expected something to happen, but nothing. The day passed.

The next morning I got on the job with the feeling I was walking into a minefield. Somehow we managed to work around each other and finished up. Kelso and I went in different directions for our next jobs. Still nothing! After a week I began to question if anything really happened, or if it was just a bad dream. We passed each other daily at the clockhouse. At the department meetings, Bill was as obnoxious as ever, but our eyes never met. I now seemed to be invisible to him. This suited me fine.

Weeks rolled into months and I marveled at how much happier I was without Bill hammering on me. Life was good, and I enjoyed it.

An affable young apprentice came to work with me around this time. We became instant friends. He enjoyed working with young kids, and became involved with me in some of my Cub Scout den projects. One day he told me that Wild Bill had an antique bottle collection. He had personally seen it and thought our young boys would just love it. He wanted to ask Bill to bring it to our next meeting.

"Good luck," I told him and dismissed the thought from my head.

About two days later I was working at the Duo Mill. It was around ten o'clock in the morning, a time we refer to as "coffee time." I walked toward the trailer. I felt my heart jump a beat! Wild Bill was steering a collision course with me. I stopped, but he kept walking at me. I thought, "O Lord, the honeymoon's over!" I kept telling myself to keep an eye on his left hand. (Bill was left-handed, you know.) He stopped a few feet from me and said something. He looked like he was waiting for a response from me. I didn't understand what he said. I was concentrating on that left hand. Then I heard "bottles" and realized he was asking how to get to our scout meeting. It seemed strange to talk to him without screaming. We were both a little awkward. We set the time and place and he left. I was shaking inside.

We held our meetings in a church hall. The night of the meeting I had the boys working on a project. I kept checking my watch. Seven-thirty, no

Bill. Eight o'clock, no Bill. I should have known he wouldn't show. Before I moved onto something else, I had one of the boys check outside again. He said there was a man out there. When I looked out the door, there was Wild Bill standing in the cold smoking a cigarette. I invited him in. Bill impressed me with his knowledge and the patience he had with the kids. It turned out to be a great meeting, and the boys really took to Bill.

The following morning at work, I went over and told him how much everyone enjoyed his presentation, and I sincerely thanked him. After this time we began to talk back and forth a little more freely, although at times it may have sounded more like grunts and whispers. As the weeks went past, some resemblance of mutual respect crept into our conversations.

I was working at the No. 10 tin line one day when I spotted Wild Bill walking down the mill. He walked over to me and said it was his last day of work. He was retiring as of the first of the month. He was wearing an "honorary" white hard hat with his name on it. It was a present to him from the office personnel. (Only foreman could wear white hats in the mills.) I shook Bill's hand and wished him well. I asked if he was going to make it a point to see every man in our department before he went home that day.

"Hell no," he bellowed, "I ain't got no use for the SOB's. I'm only seeing the people who I consider my friends. And I don't consider a man my friend until I've had a fight with him. I consider you my friend."

He said he reserved three tables at the Rainbow go-go bar on the main highway outside the plant and was inviting only his friends. He was picking up the tab and asked me to come.

"I'll be there," I said.

There were about twenty co-workers present that night. The tables were set up on a raised platform in a corner of the room. In some strange fashion I felt honored to be with Wild Bill on that night. The honored host was the life of the party. There was a lot of kidding and laughter. I watched Bill, and I was happy for him.

Later that evening, something very strange happened. Bill changed. Or was it me who changed? Either way, Wild Bill didn't look like a devil, anymore. No, sir! The man that I was looking at was an eagle!

Ma Beth

Kathi Wellington Dukes

Judy Miller, we recall
down a coke oven silo she did fall.
Judy Miller, we recall
twelve years we've missed you, one and all.

Donna Stearns, it's sad to say
that same silo snuffed her breath away.
Donna Stearns, it's sad to say
didn't live to see her children play.

Jim Soda, what a shame!
fell to his death on an overhead crane.
Jim Soda, what a shame!
Number One Roll Shop's not the same.

Jim Stout, we'll always care
died for the price of a railroad flare.
Jim Stout we still do care,
still can't see those trains out there.

Ron Clarke, Ma Beth's new prey,
thrown to his death at work today.
Ron Clarke, Ma Beth's new prey,
shouldn't have had to die that way.

Ma Beth, we're keeping score.
Twenty-four lives and you'll get no more.
Ma Beth, we're keeping score
Deadly games we play no more.

SECTION IV: Family

Darcy and the Silly Men

Gary Markley

"How are we supposed to find out when it happens?" I asked over the crackly intercom system.

"Keep your shorts on, Peno," Stubby's voice crackled back. "He promised to call right before he went in and just as soon as he can after it's over."

"Hey, I don't mind telling you guys I'm a little worried. They left at nine o'clock last night and it's four in the morning now," I said into the mike, and then headed over to start banding up a coil that had just come off the line.

"Damn! Stop worrying so much, man," Frenchie said, standing at the control panel that operated the exit end of the machinery on the tin line. "We all know how this stuff works. Hell, you've been through it two times yourself."

I knew Frenchie was right, but it had been at least 10 years since any of us had experienced this sort of thing. So why shouldn't I have felt a little apprehension? It was their first time! You'd have thought they could at least call to tell us they were all right.

Giving the bander's trigger a good pull, its hydraulics came to life and crimped the metal clip that held the steel bands around the coil. Stepping back, I waved to the craneman and headed back to Frenchie's station.

Frenchie was pulling and stroking the right side of his moustache like he always does when he's nervous. His dark brown eyes darted around like he was looking for something special.

Damn, I thought to myself. *I've known him for years and I don't think he's gained a pound over the one hundred and forty he said he hired in at. Wish I could say that! I feel as big as one of those freighters that travel the lakes bringing in coils and slabs to the Port of Indiana.*

I noticed Frenchie was getting a little gray behind the ears.

"Hey, Frenchie. There seems to be a slight dusting of snow on that jet-black roof of yours," I said, moving my head around to see his hair from different angles.

"I've got some on my ass too. Wanna see?"

"Well, I knew it couldn't be on your nuts, since you're not man enough yet to have hair on your balls," I said. Then we faked throwing punches at each other for a few seconds.

"I would have killed you with those body punches, man," he said, running his hands up and down his abdomen as though he had a washboard stomach. "No self-respecting Latino would walk around with a gut like you got."

"Would this Latino also be the kind that could at least speak Spanish to his countrymen?" I said.

Frenchie got a big smile on his face and we put in another round of fake punching.

I remember Frenchie's first day. The boss brought him into Stubby's booth where we were lining up the coils to run.

"Gentlemen," the boss said sweeping his left arm toward Frenchie, "I would like you to meet your new line mate, Javier Martinez." Using the same arm bit toward us, the boss said, "Javier, this is Justin Stockwell and Dale Banks."

"From now on, you can just call me Stubby," Dale said. Stubby then started speaking what was mumbo jumbo to me, even though I knew it was Spanish. He later told me he said welcome and that he hoped we could all get along. Javier looked confused and said, "I don't speak any Spanish."

Stubby took off his helmet and cautiously scratched his head so as not to loosen the hairspray that would make his hair drop down two feet to his side. "I have to say I'm surprised," he said.

"I can speak French very well, though," Javier said and he went into his mumbo jumbo of stuff I didn't understand. That was it. He became Frenchie from that point on.

No problem figuring out Dale's nickname. At a towering five feet five and weighing in at around two fifty with short, stout legs and arms, Stubby just has to be his name. Stubby tries to do that comb-over thing with his thinning, gray hair. He takes grief constantly from us for it, but he deals with it. I told the guys one day that you should see how long his twenty hairs have to be to go over the top, along the side, and then across the back of his head to the starting point. He was in the shower, I told them, and on one side of his head was two-inch hair and on the other side it hung down his back to his ass!

I was just plain Justin back then. I got my nickname from a food-related incident of all things. From time to time someone's wife will make an extra batch of whatever they're cooking so that we can bring it in for the whole crew to enjoy. My wife has done lasagna, chili and Buffalo wings in the past. Stubby's wife makes great corned beef and cabbage, and dishes with hunks of different sausages. One day Frenchie announced that his wife Isabel was making a batch of what we think he called pichintos. Frenchie said they're like a hot dog in a burrito and you can pour a nice taco sauce over them if you choose.

"Sounds good to me," I said. "I ain't eating anything tomorrow so I can pig out."

Frenchie should have spent a little more time telling us about his wife. As it turns out, Isabel is a Cuban straight off the island. They apparently love to cook with items that cause your tongue to catch fire. Isabel apparently felt that if her guests weren't sitting there with sweat coming off their foreheads and downing a lot of wine, she had cheated on the duties of being a hostess. Well, by the time Frenchie checked the crock pot for the tenth time and announced dinner was served, I was starved. I slapped two of those babies on half my plate and put the taco saucy stuff on the other.

In an act of pure gluttony, I grabbed a pichinto in each hand, dipped the ends in the sauce, and took a huge bite out of the left one first, followed by one out of the right one.

"Mmmmmmmmmmmm, these things taste as good as they smell. I'm going to eat ten of these things," I boasted. Then a funny sensation came over me. I'm sure I can't explain it properly, but it felt like my esophagus, starting at my stomach, was melting away upwards toward my throat.

I had never felt my mouth numb like that before. I never had anything burn so much that even water couldn't cool it off. As I found out the hard way, I never tried jalapeño peppers before. Isabel had crammed the pichintos full of them and even the sauce contained them. I needed to use asbestos toilet paper for the next two days. Thus became the legend of "Peno" Stockwell.

The last guy on our crew is Harry "Skin" Douglas. He was the one that was driving us—or at least me—nuts waiting for his call. Harry joined us last year at the ripe old age of 22. I was the only one standing there when the boss brought him in and introduced us. I told him he could call me Peno from now on.

"Looking a little bewildered, he finally said, "Peno?"

"Don't worry," I said. "One of the other bastards will be more than happy to tell you all about it."

Removing his helmet, Harry asked me how to adjust the liner so it would fit tighter. I was somewhat shocked to see that he had almost as little hair as Stubby. He had a small tuft of hair at the front and then the rest of the top of his head was bald. His blonde hair on the sides was trimmed pretty short. Trying not to gawk, I took his helmet and showed him how to make the liner slide open and close. As he was trying to operate the liner, Frenchie and Stubby came back from the food machines.

"Here come the rest of the guys," I told Harry as I pointed in their direction.

"Frenchie, Stubby . . . Harry." Before I could say anything else, Frenchie reached up and rubbed the top of Harry's head and said, "Harry? Looks more like to skin to me!" He started laughing.

"Nobody would know better than me," Stubby said and he took off his hat to show his crop. "That's definitely skin, not hair."

A few awkward moments went by, but before long everybody was laughing and it was obvious that Harry was going to fit right in. Less obvious to Harry was the fact that he was forever going to be called Skin.

"Damn it, Stubby. The shift is almost over and not a word yet," I said.

"Babies don't know anything about agendas, Peno," Stubby said. "It'll come when it's good and ready."

I didn't remember having this much trouble. My wife said, "Shit!" real loud one day and when I went to see what the problem was, she was standing in a puddle. Six hours later I was holding my daughter. My son was even quicker. He arrived about the same time we hit the emergency room door at the hospital.

Because all of our kids were at least ten years old, we had all been looking forward to this day. Strange as it may seem, the three of us are baby freaks. We hadn't had the chance to goo-goo talk in years. Our kids were at the point where they spent more time playing with friends than us. Plus, it meant Skin could join us in the kid talk. He seemed to feel left out when we passed pictures around and started telling stories about our kids.

"How was work today, hon?" my wife yelled from the kitchen when I got home.

"It stunk!" I called out as I hung up my jacket.

She yelled something I couldn't hear.

"What?" I said.

"I said, why did it stink?"

"I waited all night for Skin to have his kid and it ain't happened yet," I said

"I'm stunned that Harry hasn't had a nervous breakdown the way all you guys have been on him about his kid."

"We've just been trying to prepare him for fatherhood," I said as I entered the kitchen. I gave her a peck on the cheek. My two darlings were fighting at the breakfast table, as usual.

"It is not!"

"Is so!"

"Is not, booger face!"

"Yes, it is, spazilla!"

"Dad! He called me spazilla!"

"What seems to be the problem, booger face?" I asked as I sat down to read the paper.

"Mom made Karen's pancake bigger than mine!" Adam whined. He held his plate next to his sister's so I could make a size comparison.

"Well, it is bigger," I said, pinching the end of my chin like I was in deep-thinking mode. "There's no doubt about it now, Adam. I would have to say it appears that Mommy likes Karen best!"

Adam sat back, unable to figure out his next move and Karen stuck her tongue at him.

"Oh knock it off you two!" I said in my stern daddy voice. "Adam, Mom has enough pancake batter to make you fifty pancakes so quit whining and ask for another one."

I finished scanning the front page. "Maybe I should go to the hospital," I said.

"He'll call you when it comes, Gary," my wife said. "Don't be a weirdo."

"He might have lost my number or forgot it."

"We're in the book. Go to sleep. You look beat."

"Yeah, yeah."

"When I get home, you'll be in bed, right?" she said.

"Yes, honey!"

She hustled the kids out the door to drop them off at school.

As I walked through the automatic doors, I couldn't help notice the smell that only hospitals can produce. A receptionist smiled and said, "Do you know where you're going?"

"Yes, ma'am! Right into the old dog house when I get home!" I shuffled past her, turned left and walked down the hall toward the maternity ward.

There they were.

"What the hell are you assholes doing here?" I said, amused by our common stupidity.

"I was worried he might have lost my number," Stubby said.

"I got caught by a big train on the way home, and I was worried I missed his call," Frenchie said.

We were stuck behind a big wooden door that leads to the maternity ward. It had one small ten-by-ten inch window that was so high I had to stand on tiptoes to see through it. The guys told me they hadn't seen Skin yet, so we took turns looking for him.

Twenty minutes later Stubby yelled, "There he is!"

I cracked open the big door and yelled to Skin. He was wearing a yellow cloth gown that tied in the back and some kind of cloth overshoes. He scurried over and walked through the door.

"God, you look like shit," Frenchie told him.

"It's been terrible," Skin said. "She's been in labor for hours and she's getting madder and madder at me! I don't know what to do, other than stay out of her sight."

A short man in the same kind of gown stuck his head through the door.

"Let's go, Mr. Douglas," he said. "It's showtime."

We cheered and patted Skin on the back and high-fived each other.

Five minutes later we saw them wheel Gayle past the window with Skin walking next to her. She had on a cloth shower cap and was covered with blankets. Only her face was exposed. We cheered again and fought to peer through the window to give her the thumbs-up sign.

Gayle looked pale and totally freaked out. She turned and said something to Skin. Then she turned again and glared at us. Skin had a hangdog look on his face and gave us a weak wave, and then they disappeared through a set of double doors.

"She didn't seem too happy that we're here, did she?" Frenchie said.

"Why would she?" Stubby snapped. "She's in agony and on the way to give birth and here comes a bunch of guys cheering like they're at a sporting event."

"We'll make it up to her later, guys," I said.

We didn't have to wait long before Skin flung open the big wooden door.

"It's a girl!" he shouted. "A beautiful girl. I gotta get back. They're going to clean her up and take her measurements."

We briefly looked at one another and then proceeded to jump all over Skin. We followed him to the nursery where a nurse was cleaning off the baby. The nurse looked up through the glass and said, "Who's the father?"

"Until we get the DNA tests back, he is," Stubby said with a grin, pointing at Skin.

Skin rolled his eyes and got red-faced. The nurse handed him a card with all the information about the baby's measurements.

"You and Gayle make great kids, Skin," Frenchie said.

"Yeah, she's gorgeous, Skin," I added.

"How is Gayle doing by the way?" Stubby asked.

"She did better than I thought she would. She has to stay in the recovery room for about an hour, then she can go to her regular room. She wasn't too keen on your cheering section, I'm afraid, though."

"Yeah, we know," Stubby said. "We'll make it up to her, but tell her we're sorry when you see her."

The nurse finally gives Skin his daughter to hold. I'm totally jealous of the look of sheer joy on his face.

"She's a superstar, Skin," Frenchie said.

Another nurse walked up and told Skin that Gayle was awake and wanted to see him.

"Hot damn, gimme my baby!" Stubby said.

"You bums be careful with her!" Skin said pointing his finger at us.

"Yeah, yeah," Stubby said. "Go see mommy. We got it covered here." We formed a tight huddle around Stubby and reached out to caress the baby's tiny fingers.

"Who's the good baby?" Stubby cooed. "Are you the good baby? Are you? Yes, you're the good baby. Hey she's looking at me!"

"She's looking at your hair Stubby, trying to figure out how she could have more than you at birth," Frenchie said.

"Stop hoarding the kid, Stubby," I said, reaching for her.

I had forgotten how light babies are. And how good they smell. I almost started crying as memories of Karen and Adam's births came rushing back to me like visual echoes. What an honor to have a friend who let us share this moment with him, not that we gave him much choice.

"Time's up. Hand Starla over to Uncle Frenchie."

"Starla?" I said.

"Yeah, that's what I'm calling her. Come on, Starla. Let's go make fun of all the other babies." He carried her around a corner to a window where you could see all the babies in their little mobile cribs.

"Hey, Peno, come here," Frenchie calls in amazement. "Someone gave birth to a Clydesdale!"

Stubby tells me to go ahead. He wants to call his wife to tell her where he's at.

I walked around the corner and peered in the window. I swear it looked like a fat, from head to toe, one-year-old! The card on the crib said the boy weighed 13 pounds, 10 ounces. A nurse later told me he was the second largest baby born at that hospital. Lengthwise, he barely fit in the crib. The same nurse told me that they had to go buy diapers for a one-year-old because newborn size wouldn't fit.

"God, just imagine the noise that came out of the woman who grunted this dude out," Frenchie laughed. "Look at that baby, Starla. I bet he takes shits bigger than you, heh?"

"Nice talk," I said as I walked back around the corner. I saw Stubby hang up the phone.

"What was it?" Stubby said.

"World's largest baby," I answered. "But if you're going over there, try and be polite. It is someone's kid, you know."

"I can be tactful," Stubby assured me. Seconds later I hear Stubby's voice: "Holy fuck!"

"Where's the baby, Peno? Gayle wants to see her now," Skin said, returning from the recovery room.

"Starla's around the corner with Frenchie making fun of other babies," I said.

Skin took a step, then froze and turned back to me. "Starla?" he said.

"That's what we've been calling her."

He looked at me disapprovingly. "Hey, we could have called her Skinette!" I said, smiling.

He shook his head and continued walking to get his baby.

"Ever seen one of these, Stubby?" Frenchie said. "It's called a church."

"Up yours," Stubby said.

It was a nice ceremony. Skin's baby was christened Darcy Lynn Douglas and she handled it like a champ, never crying once. Frenchie teared up once, but said it was only because she should have been named Starla. We waited by the baptismal font as the family went back into the church to take pictures.

"Be careful, Stubby," I said, "that holy water could burn an evil bastard like you."

Frenchie laughed along with me, and Stubby pulled out one side of his coat to hide his other hand inside so he could flip us the bird.

"That does it!" Frenchie said and he dipped his fingers in the water and flicked it at Stubby.

"I'm melting . . . melting!" Stubby cried as he faked shrinking to the floor.

I heard someone say, "Who are those people?"

We looked up and saw Gayle standing next to another woman and staring at us with crossed arms. "Those are just some silly men Harry works with," she said.

"I don't think we're in her good graces yet," I whispered out of the side of my mouth wishing I could find somewhere to hide.

"Hap-py birth-day . . . to . . . you."

We clapped and cheered. Darcy looked at us like we were insane. How could this kid be a year old already? I thought. She still was one of the prettiest girls that I had ever seen. I warned Skin that she was going to be a handful come dating age.

The proud parents took turns helping Darcy open her presents and then they helped her blow out the one big candle on her cake. As is the tradition, Gayle gave Darcy a big piece of cake and allowed her to eat it her way. This, of course, was to smear it from ear to ear on her face. Everyone laughed and took pictures.

"Look, Darcy, Peno eats like you do!" Frenchie said. He picked up a slice of cake and crammed it into my mouth. I tried to get most of it in my mouth, but of course, most of it ended up on my face. We all laughed, including Darcy, and Stubby took my picture. It was somewhere around this time that I realized we were the only ones laughing.

A quick glance at Gayle told me we'd done it again. She was with two neighbor ladies who had brought their kids to Darcy's party.

"Oh, that's just the silly men that Harry works with," she forced out between her teeth.

After the party, we apologized to Harry as he walked us to our cars. "That's all right," he said softly, "I thought it was funny and so did Darcy."

It's hard enough moving a child's swing set in the light of day. Imagine trying to do it in the dead of night without waking up the neighbors.

"Lift up your end so we can get started, Peno," Stubby whispered.

"I'm trying, but the poles are stuck in the ground!"

"Outta my way, pussy," Frenchie said, trying to step in front of me. "I'll get it."

"I'll get it!" I said. I grabbed the side bar and yanked with everything I had. I jerked the poles three feet out of the ground, causing the swings to slam into the seesaw.

"For Pete's sake, Peno!" Stubby hissed. "It's two o'clock in the morning. Do you want to wake everybody up?"

"Fuck yeah," Frenchie said. "Then they can help us get this shit moved so we can go home!"

We moved the old swing set to the street where our trucks were parked. Then we set up a new swing set where the old one had been positioned. Finally, Stubby and I carried the Fisher-Price Kiddie Clubhouse to a nice flat spot and set it down.

Darcy had wanted this clubhouse real bad for her fifth birthday, but Skin said they couldn't afford it. He said Gayle wanted to get a new swing set if they were going to spend any money at all. But it turned out they couldn't afford that either.

Frenchie taped a sign on the clubhouse that read "Happy Birthday Darcy." We slowly crossed the yard to get to our trucks. Stubby tripped over a root sticking up from a lilac bush and went down like a ton of bricks.

"OUCH! Son of a bitch! Kiss my ass . . . dammit!" Stubby cried at the top of his lungs.

"Help me throw this dumb-ass in the front seat of my truck before the cops come!" Frenchie said, panic creeping into his voice. "You drive my truck."

As we pulled away, I saw the lights come on in at least three houses and I heard the sounds of Stubby cussing a blue streak.

The next night Skin came to work and was at a loss for words: "You guys are something else. I don't know what to say."

"Who cares what you have to say," I said. "How about Darcy?"

"She didn't want to come in to bed last night. She was in that clubhouse all day singing and talking on that little fake phone."

"Then it was all worthwhile," Frenchie said.

"Speak for yourself, asshole!" Stubby said. I went on to tell Skin how old sure-foot wiped out his kneecaps and woke up the neighbors.

Skin said that when Darcy hugged her mom real tight and thanked her for the clubhouse and swing set, Gayle told her that some special men who work with Daddy brought it for her because they like her a lot.

"Those silly men I'm always talking about, I told her," Skin said. "Darcy said to tell you she loves you guys," Skin said.

"Does that mean we're finally out of the doghouse with Gayle?" I asked.

"Sounded like it," he said smiling.

"Can we come to the next party?" Stubby asked.

"We'll see, but don't push it," Skin said.

Life is so unfair sometimes. No one got to go to Darcy's sixth birthday party. She was in the hospital awaiting treatment for a form of leukemia. Why do innocent little girls have to learn to understand that they have something inside of them that may kill them? Why should a kid have to be braver than any adult would want to be? What do you say to a little girl whose hair is thin and brittle from bouts with radiation? What do you say when she knows she's so thin due to the inability to keep food down? What do you say when you know, that she knows, you're scared she's gonna die?

What do you say to parents who are watching their flesh and blood wither and die?

We worked for nearly a year barely uttering a word between us. What could we say? There wasn't any joy to share. I found myself hugging my kids more when I got home. I was almost embarrassed that my life had been without any real heartache, much less something of this magnitude. I didn't know if my voice carried any weight with God, but I prayed every night for Darcy to turn the corner and start coming back to us and not further toward Him.

Thank goodness for the medical benefits at the mill. Most of the big medical expenses were covered. But after two years, even the little things started to add up to big numbers. We threw lots of benefit dinners and solicited funds wherever we could to help Skin and Gayle. They did a great job of keeping their heads above water financially, and in the third year Darcy finally started to beat the disease. It would still be a while until we could call her healthy, but knowing that she was going to live made all the difference.

We started to converse again at work about happy things. We made plans that Darcy's ninth birthday was going to be a blowout. Skin started to look human again. He had aged so much during Darcy's illness. People seem to forget that when a family member has a bad disease, they all suffer from it. Skin and Gayle were trying to get healthy again as much as their daughter was.

One day, Skin seemed down. I was worried that Darcy might not be doing well, so I had to ask what was wrong. He said Darcy was doing great, but he was worried that the bills were piling up . He said they might have to sell their house. I told him to give us another chance to see what we could do before he sold it.

We hit it hard again for another month with raffles, dinners, and asking for money. But other kids are sick, too, and the world can't stop everything to take care of one little girl and her parents, no matter how good of people they are.

Finally, the bank account they had set up for Darcy was pretty much tapped out. Now and then ten or twenty bucks would come in, but nothing to add up to the thirty thousand dollars they needed. Skin and Gayle started to make plans to sell their house and move in with her mother til they built up some cash.

I talked it over with Frenchie as we left the mill on a crisp autumn day. We agreed it was a rotten deal.

In the parking lot, I saw Frenchie's gleaming 1963 Corvette taking up two parking spots. It was his pride and joy.

"What the hell is this doing out!" I said.

"Baby wanted to stretch her legs," he said, patting the T-top and giving it a kiss.

"This is October, dude! You don't take the cover off this thing but four times a year and they're all summer days!"

"I don't know. I just felt like riding in her today."

He slipped behind the wheel and fired her up. He gave a salute with his hand and sped away. The lucky bastard was on vacation for the next two weeks. Things were pretty boring without Frenchie around. A new guy I couldn't stand filled in for him. I spent most of my time between coils looking at pictures Darcy had drawn for us.

A few days later Skin's voice echoed jubilantly over the intercom.

"Hello, tin line! How's it hanging today? Peno, meet me at Stubby's booth. You gotta hear this!"

Banding up my coil, I gave the craneman the OK to pick it up and hustled down to hear the news.

"Just when I figure we've used up every miracle we've been allotted, another falls from the sky!" he said.

"Come on, come on," I said, flustered. "Tell us the news!"

"The bank called yesterday and the account has another twenty thousand plus in it!" he said. He looked like he was going to jump up and down. "We don't have to sell the house after all!"

Life had finally come back full-circle. Darcy's party was coming up. Skin's house was safe, and it was going to be fun to come to work again. Thank you, God.

I promised Skin I would deliver the birthday invitation to Frenchie since I wanted to tell him the good news anyway. I grabbed a six-pack after work and headed for Frenchie's place. I practically floated up his front steps to tell him the good news.

He opened the door.

"Here's an invitation to a beautiful woman's party," I said. "And here's a six-pack for being a stunningly handsome man with great taste in cars and friends. Now let me in so I can tell you the big news, Javier my friend!"

We always had to call Frenchie "Javier" around his wife, Isabel, or she would have a shit fit—a big whooping Cuban shit fit. I came inside and asked if he wanted to go to the garage where we usually set up a couple of folding chairs to drink beer. We did this to avoid making a mess inside, thus avoiding Isabel's wrath.

Frenchie said we could talk in the living room. I laid it all out for him, how everything had finally worked out for Skin and Gayle. I told him that it was going to be like old times when we were all happy. We were victorious! Frenchie seemed really happy, yet something just wasn't ringing true in his voice.

Isabel walked into the living room. She gave Frenchie a look that made me wish I was headed out the door. He sort of tipped his head and gave her some eyebrow action that seemed to indicate, "Don't start something."

She ignored him and cracked off something in Spanish.

"Don't start with me, Isabel!" he snarled. "I'm not going to listen to your bitching!"

I started slowly backing toward the door and potential freedom from what I thought was going to be a big one. She called him "estupido" something and said he should try and make her so happy, whatever that meant.

"Shut up, Isabel!" Frenchie screamed.

Fuck the front door. The garage door was closer. As I slipped into the garage and closed the door behind me I heard the only word I recognized from Isabel's stream of broken English . . . "Corvette!"

I turned on the lights and looked for Frenchie's golf clubs. I had the distinct feeling that I might have to protect the Vette from Isabel. As I looked over Isabel's green Mustang, I saw an empty space. The Vette was gone! The cloth tarp that was always draped over it was folded up and sitting on a shelf. The spare set of tires and box of impossible-to-find spare parts were also gone! What the hell?

It dawned on me just as Frenchie walked through the garage door. His head was down, and he didn't seem to know what to say.

"You sold the Vette?"

"Yeah. It was more trouble than it was worth."

"What did you get for it?"

"Enough."

"So, what did you do with the money?"

"I invested it in a good deal. Listen, I never want to talk about it again, and I don't want to hear you talking about it either."

"You are the most amazing man I've ever met, Javier Ramón Martinez," I said and shook his hand.

"Shut up and get us a beer out of the fridge," he barked in mock anger.

Darcy wanted what every other kid wanted that year—a Furby. A Furby is an electronic talking animal that was that year's Cabbage Patch Kid or Elmo doll. So it was next to impossible to find one for a kid whose birthday comes shortly after Christmas.

I don't know how we did it, but we all showed up with a Furby for Darcy. Skin was amazed because he'd had no luck in finding one. Skin also found out from the bank what Frenchie had done. It took a lot of pleading, but I convinced him not to let Frenchie know what they had found out.

Darcy looked adorable. You would never have known she was sick. Boy did she love those Furbies! She wouldn't put them down even while we had cake and ice cream. After we sat around talking for a while, Gayle said, "Darcy, would you like to thank everyone for the nice gifts you got?"

She thanked her parents, her grandparents, her aunt and uncle, the neighbors and her friends. Then she looked at us sitting on the couch and said, "But I like you guys the most cause you brought me Furbies!"

"Do you remember their names, Darcy?" Gayle asked.

"Yes," she said. "Peno, Stubby, and Frenchie—the silly men that Dad works with!"

"No, they aren't silly," Gayle said smiling at us. "They've been your guardian angels since you were born. Let's thank them properly."

She took Darcy's hand and came over to me first.

"This angel's name is Justin," she told Darcy. "Thank you, Justin," Gayle said and then she kissed my cheek.

"Thank you, Angel Justin," Darcy said and kissed my other cheek.

"You're very welcome, Darcy," I said, trying not to cry. I watched Gayle as she told Darcy about Angel Dale and Angel Javier. I watched as they did their best to stay calm as they got their kisses.

Darcy saved us from making sobbing fools of ourselves when she said, "Daddy, aren't you going to thank the angels?"

Frenchie perked right up.

"Yeah, Daddy, come get some!" he said as he held out his arms and puckered his lips out. I took pictures of Skin kissing Stubby and Frenchie. Everyone laughed their heads off. The moment was too special to share immediately, but I knew someday the pictures would be priceless when I hung them up for everyone on the line to see.

It was a nice way to start the new year. Tomorrow when we go back to work, we'll be starting our new project. Skin wants to brainstorm some ideas to make money. We figure if we work a little throughout the next five years, we could have enough to buy Frenchie a new Vette! That should be just perfect since he will be having a mid-life crisis at that time. What will make a man feel young and virile again better than a Vette? Frenchie's gonna shit!

Men of Steel, Hearts of Gold

P. David Woodring

My grandfather was the first man of steel. He came to Baltimore straight from the hills of West Virginia looking for a better life for his family after World War II. He found it at Bethlehem Steel's Sparrows Point Plant.

He was a tall man with a hawk-like nose and brown, leathery skin that hung off his bones like clothes on a scarecrow. He must have been a big man once, but I never remembered him that way. Pop never talked much and if he spoke at all, it was only a few words.

Pop worked at the cold mill, and somehow he always worked days with weekends off. He would come and get us on Friday night to spend the weekend with him. I liked to go with Pop, though he never said much. He would take us to the plant to pick up his check. He always cashed it at a liquor store in Edgemere, where he would buy a half-pint of Seagram's Seven, a big bag of Utz potato chips, and a Coca-Cola for us. Then we would go to his house.

He lived in Bayshore Trailer Park. His mobile home was right on the water. You could see the steel mill from there. There was a huge weeping willow in his backyard. That's where Pop would squat on his haunches and drink his bottle and sleep. I never figured out how he managed to do that without falling over. My brother and I would fish and crab all day. Pop would rouse only to remove a hook from a finger or a fish, untangle a fishing line, or untangle my brother and me from a fight. Maybe he wasn't asleep.

In the summer, Pop always had watermelon. He would go to Cheap Charlie's on the Boulevard and get them five for a dollar. Every boy and girl in the neighborhood would be at Pop's for watermelon. He always sliced them longways so you got a nice big wedge. He never yelled about the seed fights, but Pop never had much to say. I remember the cold juices from the melon trickling down my plump belly, making tracks in the dirt on my stomach from a hard day of playing. It never mattered how hot it was; Pop always wore long underwear. I would stand there soaked with sweat and dirt babies ringing my neck while Pop squatted in his regular spot, sound asleep, without a drop of perspiration on his brow.

Sometimes Pop and I would sit on the end of the pier in the fleeting moments between daylight and darkness when time seemed to stand still. The water lapped softly against the pilings and the smell of creosote—cooked out of the wood from the heat of the summer—hung in the air. I dangled my feet in the water and he squatted there like an ancient Indian, quiet and solemn.

We always faced the west looking out across the bay toward Sparrows Point. An eerie calm pervaded as the sun set behind the mill. The last rays filtered through the smog and dust particles creating a beautiful collage of colors. But the mill, it never stopped. In the distance, you could hear the rumble of heavy machinery, the clink and clunk of steel on steel, and the occasional blast of a horn from a locomotive or a mill calling men back to their jobs. I never asked Pop what he thought about while we were out there. Not because I didn't think he would tell me, but because I was afraid to break the spell.

Some years later, I asked my dad what he thought Pop might have been thinking and Dad didn't hesitate: "Those were the best times of his life—the time he spent with you guys. Working at Bethlehem Steel, he made more money there in a week than sometimes he used to make in a year. And he knew he would get paid. Pop didn't think it could be any better."

Everybody in the trailer park had a cat, except Pop. We had to pull the crab lines out of the water at night to keep the crabs from eating the bait. But then the cats would be after the bait. Pop was the general and my brother and I were his cavalry. When Pop heard those damn cats, he would send us charging out to the pier armed with brooms to sweep the cats into the water. That was the most fun of all, except that by the end of the summer, I think those cats liked the water. If they couldn't dodge around us, they jumped into the river before we got the chance to whack them with our brooms.

I learned a lot from Pop. Every curse word I know, I'd heard Pop say. I practiced regularly with my brother.

Once when I was about eight years old, Pop was squatting in his regular sleeping spot. Unsure if he was awake or not, I said, "Hey, Pop, how about I have a drink of that bottle?"

He handed me the bottle without saying anything. I had me a healthy swig of his whiskey. My eyes watered, my stomach burned and my face felt flush. Pop let me smoke cigarettes and chew tobacco with him too. He taught me how to inhale, and man, did it make me dizzy! When he gave me a chaw of his Red Man, I got really sick and threw up. He must have forgotten to tell me not to swallow. To this day, I have no taste for hard liquor or tobacco of any kind. Pop taught me more than I thought.

He taught me some good things too, like tying my shoes. And he bought me my first watch after he taught me to tell time. It was a Big Ben pocket watch he bought at the hardware store for five dollars.

Pop finally retired from the mill and moved to Boiling Springs, North Carolina. We went to see him as often as we could, but I sure missed him. Pop wasn't feeling well and finally, my dad got him to go to the doctor.

When Pop came back, he wasn't even in the door yet when Granny announced: "Guess what everybody, Pop has cancer!" Granny never did have much tact.

I was pretty upset, but Pop told me not to worry because he knew he had cancer long before the damn doctor told him. He went downhill pretty quick after that and we all took turns sitting with him. Pop was so sick, he couldn't even go to the bathroom by himself. He had to ask me to help him. That alone was enough to kill him. But I didn't mind. The very last thing I remember Pop saying to me was "Ain't this a hell of a thing?" He never did say much, and for the first time I was sure Pop was sleeping.

My father was born in November 1929, right after the Roaring Twenties and just in time for the Great Depression. Times were hard and he never had much as a child growing up. Dad's grandfather and his father, my Pop, made some of the best corn liquor in Wirt County during the Prohibition. Unfortunately, Great-Grand Pap and Pop were selling more liquor than the sheriff and the preacher.

At a pie social at the church, they decided to ask Pop to quit selling his liquor in town. Dad said he remembers the fight well. He was only five but he said the two of them were really working Pop over and he cut one of them with a knife. They never found that knife—my dad said it was hidden in a hot water bottle—but Pop still went to prison for five years. When he got out, the war had started and he joined up to fight. I guess this was all too much for Granny. She left my dad and his brother in an orphanage. They stayed there for almost five years.

I asked my dad how he felt being left in that home. He said it wasn't so bad. He said he got a good education and a roof over his head. Dad said he was probably better off there than he would have been otherwise.

Great Grand Pap would get my dad and his brother in the summers. Finally, he came to get the boys for good, only they wouldn't let him have them. So he came back the next day with a shotgun and took them home. The sheriff paid Grand Pap a visit to collect the boys. My dad said Great Grand Pap told the sheriff, "You can get your ass back up the road while you can still walk, or someone can carry you out with a load of buckshot in it." The sheriff never came back.

They lived with Great Grand Pap till Pop came home from the war and took them to Baltimore.

My dad was the second man of steel. He went to work for Bethlehem in 1947 and spent the next thirty-seven years working in the tin mill, first in the pickler, then as millwright with the mechanical gang. Dad was always a union man. He said back then you could join the union for two dollars, but you didn't say anything about it because the union wasn't strong enough yet and you could get fired for belonging.

Dad met and married my mom a couple years after he came to Baltimore, I think it was June of 1949. Somehow, Pop and Granny had gotten back together during the war. Granny had known my mother's stepmother back in West Virginia and told them there was opportunity for work in Baltimore. And one day they just showed up at Pop's.

The first time my dad laid eyes on my mom, he had just come off a night shift at the mill. In fact, her whole family was there. Dad would tell this story with that cross-tooth smile of his and look at my mom with a glint in his eye. "She was like a bloodhound on the trail of a convict," he would say. There wasn't any way he was getting away from her, so he married her. They had two children before me: my sister, Brenda, and my brother, Bill. I was the baby. Dad always said I was an accident—the best one he ever had.

From the time I could walk, I followed Dad everywhere. I guess he didn't mind much cause he took me wherever he went. My dad walked with his toes pointing out. I know because when I followed him I tried to imitate his walk. Where he stepped, I stepped.

Dad was just a plain-looking man. He had a head of coal-black hair that he normally kept cropped short. But whenever it got the least bit long, he had a cowlick in the front and it would curl down on his forehead. I guess that's why he kept it short. When he came home from The Point, I liked to climb on his lap and run my hands through his bristly hair and kiss his rough, unshaven face. When he smiled, one of his front teeth kind of overlapped the other one. I always hoped mine would overlap too, but when I got my permanent teeth, Dad said it probably wouldn't happen.

My dad was a man of steel and his hands were proof. They were big strong hands: hands that worked with tools. Hands of steel. And yet they were gentle hands. Hands that nurtured. Hands that taught. Hands that brushed over a sick boy's forehead in the middle of the night and made everything all right.

My dad and I used to go to the airport when I was very young. He was a private pilot and we would go to Eastern Airport where he kept his plane. Dad owned a 1939 Aeronka Chief. It was a two-person plane where you sat side by side. Dad bought that plane for three hundred dollars. Someone had torn the wing off so we re-covered the wings in my mom's living room and did the rest of the fuselage on the porch.

Sometimes we would go up for a ride and other times we would just hang around the airport and talk with the guys. I liked sitting in the airplane beside my dad. He would strap me in and I would pull the magneto while he spun the prop and the engine would come to life.

We would go up and I would ask Dad to fly by Sparrows Point. It was quite a sight in those days. They were still making steel the old way. Dad said there were over thirty thousand people working there then. If we flew over at shift change, the workers looked like ants coming and going to the anthill. Sparrows Point was in its glory days then. It was the early '60s and production was in full swing. The blast furnace and the open hearth were going full-steam, belching and spewing smoke and gases into the air. The coke ovens were still working and blue fire shot from the stacks as the coke gasses were burned off. I used to want to fly right over but Dad said you never fly over a smokestack because something could fly into the air and hit the plane.

Our house was small. It was built during the war as temporary housing for people working at Martin Marietta. Dad was always adding onto that house. First it was a porch that became a bedroom, and then a porch behind that, and it went on and on. One day we went to the lumberyard to get some building supplies. Out in the yard, a couple of young men had made a pair of stilts. They tried to walk on them but didn't know how. Dad said, "Let me see them," and walked all around the yard on them. They were amazed. "Man, he's ten foot tall," one of them said. I was amazed that he could walk on stilts, but to me he was always ten feet tall. He was a man of steel and there wasn't anything he couldn't do.

Dad wouldn't work any overtime at the mill. He always said you get used to living on the extra money and when it's not there, what are you going to do then? Most of the families in the neighborhood saved all year to go to Ocean City for a week, but not us. Dad wanted us to see this great country we live in and I can tell you that we saw most of it. By the time I was thirteen, I had been from Florida to Maine and all up through Canada and most of the Midwest, as well as some of the Southwest.

We didn't go first-class. I mean, we didn't stay in motels or eat in restaurants. Dad built us a tent camper long before Coleman ever built their first one. We got the directions out of *Popular Mechanics.*

Dad never owned a new car. Most people wouldn't even drive to work in the car that we used to see the country. It was an old blue Ford station wagon. The quarter fenders were rusted and the paint was faded. The car had a red tint from the iron oxide that coated everything at Sparrows Point back then. Dad never worried about the car breaking down. If it did, he just fixed it. He was a man of steel.

Once we were vacationing with my uncle and his family. We stopped to eat. My uncle took his family into a restaurant while we ate sandwiches from the cooler in the parking lot. I threw a fit. I wanted to eat in the restaurant. What I didn't realize was that my dad had just enough money in his pocket to get us home, plus a little extra for an emergency. Now, as an adult, I think back on how much we did as a family and realize the sacrifices my parents made to give us those experiences. I'm humbled at my father's capacity for love and giving after having had so little as a child himself.

When I got married, Dad was my best man. He had broken his leg in a motorcycle accident and had a cast up to his hip. I wouldn't have had anyone else as my best man.

I'm the third man of steel. I never planned on working at the mill and I don't think my father ever wanted me to. Not that the mill hadn't been good to him. But every father has bigger dreams for his son. Dad wanted me to go to college and I tried. But I guess I wasn't ready for it.

For twenty years I worked for myself, driving tractor-trailers. But the funny thing is, that even while doing that, I couldn't get away from Bethlehem Steel. I was either hauling the finished product from the mill or bringing raw materials in.

The job had gotten old and one day I was loading steel and complaining that if I could sell my truck and get a job at the mill, I would do it. Nancy, the lady in shipping, told me that Bethlehem was hiring truck drivers. Dad always said, "Don't run your mouth if you can't back it up," so here I am today, working in the mill's mobile equipment division.

I have children of my own now. My daughter, Kelly, is the oldest and I have a son, Ryan. Ryan has been spending more time with my dad lately. They go to air shows and sometimes they go to "old goat" meetings at the airport. That's what Ryan calls them. Ryan says Dad is the oldest one there.

Ryan and I were at my dad's the other day. Dad was helping Ryan build a wind tunnel for a science project. It had snowed that day. Dad walked us to the car, like he always insists on doing.

I kissed my dad's rough, unshaven face and ran my fingers through his salt and pepper hair. "You never get too big to kiss your dad," my dad always says. Looking over his shoulder where the three of us had walked to the car, I noticed there was only one set of footprints, toes pointing out.

I looked closely, and there inside the larger footprints was a smaller set of prints. I hope Ryan won't be the fourth man of steel. But then, men of steel have hearts of gold.

The Watch

J.A. Orellana

I was awarded my "Twenty-five Years"
watch.
It seems so solitary—
A pocket watch engraved with my name.
A dog tag with a heart telling me
how many years of my life have died
in the mill.
There was no fanfare, no drinks or prayers,
no funeral or condolences given.
Just the watch, like a flag given to a mother
after her son's death at war.
And I mourn as she does her son—
I mourn every one of those twenty-five years.
Papa, I wish you were here with me
to give them a proper sendoff.
We would buy a bottle of Canadian
Mist,
toast through the night into the dawn,
recalling each of my children.
All twenty-five of them.
We would place them side by side in a canoe,
raise a white sheet on the mast,
drench everything with gas,
light it, and push it into the sea.
Together we would sit wrapped
in a blanket
until the canoe would melt lavender
with the horizon.
We would do like the Vikings did
with their heroes.
But since that cannot be, I toast you
Papa.
I can still see you drifting lavender
into the horizon amidst
my lacking you.

Alan Kepler

Joe Gutierrez

Alan Kepler had just signed his retirement papers. He had five days to go and they scheduled him midnights. Everybody was pissed but Alan. He couldn't have cared less. "What's one more week of midnights," he laughed. "Been working them all my life."

They could have scheduled him days that last week and let him just walk around like they do for some people. "Makes no difference," he said. "When I walk out those doors Friday morning, we're on our way to New Orleans and they can kiss my behind."

I don't think I ever heard him cuss, except when somebody did something really dumb. Then he might say, "Damn." For the life of me, I can't remember his face. But I remember his eyes. They were blue and they smiled. He was a gentle man, and that's what I remember. That and the sometimes funny jokes he tried to tell.

Alan was fifty-five years old, but with his white receding hair and his slow walk, he seemed much older. His hands were gnarled with arthritis. He said he soaked them for hours in hot paraffin wax. Then he'd laugh and say it didn't help much, but it took his mind off his knees which weren't much better.

His back ached like all the old backs in the Galvanize Department, especially when he had to skim the heavy, hot slag off the surface of the molten zinc melted to the eight hundred and fiftieth degree. The long, ninety-pound iron spoons wreaked havoc on old tendons and weak, calcium-deprived bones.

It all added up to pain, but Al never really complained. The guys who worked with him never complained either. Al did his job the best he could. But there was a lot he couldn't do, and most everybody went out of their way to help him. He told me once that we go as far as we can go, then God takes us the rest of the way.

I never thought about that too much, until later.

Alan bought a motor home and planned to roam the country. The whole department knew every detail about that house on wheels. He told us every move he made, from the day he ordered it to the day he picked it up. He duct-taped a picture of himself and his wife standing in front of his "Escape to Paradise" on one wall of the operator's booth. On the other wall, he taped a twenty-by-twenty inch Standard Oil map of the U.S.A and highlighted Route 66 and Route 41. He promised to send post cards to everyone who asked and even to those he didn't like, just to let them know he was thinking of them.

He was excited and it was overflowing and it was beautiful and we were happy for him. We listened to his dreams and we became part of them, thinking along that someday we'd be there too. Someday.

We smiled when he talked about how he was going to stand on the rim of the Grand Canyon with his arms around his wife and watch the sun melt into the horizon. He said that he had never seen Boulder Dam, but he was going to. Al loved to fish, and his eyes glistened when he talked about fishing off Cape Cod and the Florida Keys. He said he planned on fishing until he turned into a fish. He read every cookbook he could get his hands on and said he was going to cook fish every way it could be cooked and eat it morning, noon and night.

Big Mike Bochenek was probably his best buddy. He would laugh and say, "Take me with you, Al. I ain't never seen anybody turn into a fish." For years they rode to work together in a blue Volkswagen that Al bragged got nine hundred miles to the gallon.

Yep, Alan Kepler Kessler was retiring and that was all he talked about. That and the problem with his prostate. And that bothered him more than anything else. Sam Meisterharm, strip inspector, galvanize sage, philosopher, two-fisted barroom brawler and lover of cool mint liquor, bought Al *Playboy* magazines and told him to eat ground rhinoceros horn. Sam was a little crazy. A good guy, but crazy. I told Al what a good friend had told me: "There's one thing to remember about a crazy person. He's crazy all the time; even when it seems like he's making sense."

Al talked, laughed and worked through two midnight turns. He had three to go. It was Wednesday night, April 26, a few minutes after eleven.

I was working on number three shear, when I saw Big Mike. He was walking in alone and he was late. The shift started at eleven. He asked me if I saw Al come in. I told him no. Big Mike just shook his head and kind of whispered, "Al never showed up."

The hawk was out that night and it was biting. When the truck drivers opened the frozen doors on the finishing end, the walls screamed with cold and the wind icicled its way through the stacked coils reminding everyone that winter was still here.

The salamanders were blowing hot. Number one and two lines were down. Three and four were running. Al worked on number three with Big Mike. Kepler was the assistant and Big Mike was the operator. Bochenek was from the harbor and he was tough. But he looked worried that night.

It was three in the morning when we got the news. Someone—I don't remember who—called and said that Al had been killed coming to work. Some young girl was drunk and she crossed the center line. Hit him head on. They said he was already dead when they cut him out of his blue Volkswagen. He was three blocks from home.

That night, the Galvanize Department cried.

No one removed the photograph and map. They hung there for the longest time. After awhile, the picture faded and the map became tattered. We taped it again and again. Then one day they were gone. But when March comes around pushing April and someone opens that finishing end door and a cold wind whistles through the Galvanize, I swear I can hear Alan laughing.

I close my eyes and whisper, "Enjoy your retirement, Al."

Steelworker Talking Thoughts

Gary Novotny

When all is said and done, and all the truths been told, the memories I have are these:

I see a foggy, faraway picture of a man standing in the rain. His collar is turned up against the damp chill. Smoking a cigarette, without a hat, he peers with a drilling eye into the darkness; his ocular muscle straining to see something in the inky blackness.

It's as if he's trying to look through time and into the framed images in his own memory. What is he looking for? What does he see?

Years merge. It is always night. In the inky blackness, images, thoughts, feelings, people, places and objects flip through his mind's eye like a fanned deck of picture cards held up real close.

A young lad crying: "I don't have no more pudding in my bowl, Momma!"

A small hand holding a squirt gun under a water tap.

Dirty Harry on a 24-inch J. C. Higgins bike; a red one with chrome fenders and a sleek and streamlined white center bar tank with built-in dual headlights.

A big dining room table with white tablecloth, silvery white plates, and sparkling champagne glasses partially filled with golden liquid. It's Thanksgiving or Christmas. My head comes up to my uncle's elbow as I sit next to him. He is a wiry man, hairs in his nostrils; white cuffs and silver links sticking out from his suit coat sleeves. His hands are shaped by cold gray labor. Powerful and solid.

Dad carves the meat. He is quiet and the knife is sharp. My mother is setting out cloth napkins and sterling silver cutlery. Plates are full of snowy holiday desserts, Christmas cut-out cookies, fudge, nut-roll, pumpkin pie, poppy seed roll, and egg nog. All made by my mother. How? She wanted to please. Thank you, folks, I'm so late remembering.

I hold a big round hand mirror. I look into it and see the darkness of night. In it, there is a street lamp and a man standing in the rain. His collar turned up against the chill. I am he.

I feel like crying when I think of some of these images. I don't. I hold it in. It would sound funny anyway. A sob like a honking goose.

Long Live 'D' Crew

Gary Markley

Six months on the job and I'm transferred to the galvanizing line because the boss' girlfriend wants my job.

"Damn! When are they gonna hire female supervisors so I can sleep my way to the top?" No one hears my grumbling as I walk toward my new workstation. I swing my lunch box with extra force because it makes the thermos bang loudly against the sides. I pretend the sounds are punches to my boss' face.

"Take that, you good-for-nothing-skirt-chasing-bastard," I mutter through clenched teeth as I land an imaginary uppercut that catches him under the chin.

The speaker system crackles overhead as I pass the operator's station. "New meat's coming down."

Oh great, just what I need to start the day: comedians.

Arriving at my post, I wearily greet Tommy, who's assigned to teach me the recorder's duties on the galvanizing line. A recorder's job is to take down all the information on each coil as it comes off the line. The job is basically the same on all the lines, but there are always some special quirks to be learned. That's why I'm getting trained today.

"Who's the putz that announced that new meat has arrived?" I ask.

Tommy chuckles. "Oh, that was Dozer—I mean Don Reese—at the entry end. You'll get a kick outta these guys. They're a strange group."

Our conversation is interrupted by a voice from behind. "So, who is this unfortunate fellow, Tommy?"

I turn to face a man wearing shades and a scruffy beard.

"Garrett London, your new recorder," I say in a tough-guy voice tinged with contempt. For good measure, I give him my best you-don't-scare-me stare.

The bearded guy slowly—and I mean slowly—like he wants me to anticipate his next words, cracks a long grin.

"Well, Garrett, you ain't nuttin' but a pup, but we'll learn you the ropes. I'm up in that thar crane today if you have any questions." He wipes his mouth on his sleeve as he walks away. Looking back, he shouts, "I'll watch out fer yer head today, but after that you keep a watch out fer me!"

I turn to Tommy in disbelief. "Ain't nuttin' but a *pup*? *Learn* you? That *thar* crane? You've got to be kidding me!"

"I told you it was a strange group."

A voice on the loudspeaker announces, "I saw the new guy and they sent us another puppy."

"We'll paper-train him," another voice says.

I walk slowly to the microphone so that the crew members can see me pushing the button. "Bite me, assholes!"

My training period is over and today is the first time I'll be alone with "D" crew. It will also be the first of seven consecutive midnight shifts. I never get used to working through the night. It always messes up my body clock. I struggle all night to stay awake and in the morning when I walk out the plant, the sun burns my tired eyes like fire. Once home, I fight myself to sleep when my body is ready to enjoy the day. So, if I'm lucky, I get three hours of good sleep. By the third day of these midnight turns, I'm reduced to a worthless pile of shit.

At the entry end of the line, I pick up the info cards on the first few coils we'll be running. I sort of nod hello to the two guys on the line and start down the exit end to my desk. Past the large furnace area, I come to the operator's control panel where an older man is sitting. He spins in his chair toward me and motions me over with his hand. Oh crap! Here we go. Let the bullshit commence.

"Hi, Garrett, I'm Papa Dunn."

I nod back and he begins: "Are you ready to be part of history, Garrett? We are what everybody else wishes they could be. We run prime all the time and when there is a record to set, you can damn sure believe we set it."

"I can get behind that," I tell him.

I find out later that Papa Dunn is the emotional glue that holds this band of misfits together. He's six feet tall and thin as a rail. For a man in his sixties, though, he has the thickest head of silver hair I've ever seen. His eyes and cheeks show the wrinkles of time, but overall, he seems healthy and smart as a whip. He leads quietly by example. Only when things are about to explode does he speak with an angry voice. This always ends any uprising because—and I'm not sure why—no one wants to disappoint Papa.

Papa tells me he has two simple rules: 1) You get to work on time to do your job right and, 2) You never do anything to make him push the emergency button. The emergency button is about five inches in diameter. If you push it, the whole line shuts down. It means something bad has happened. The company loses money and the crew loses incentive pay. No good comes from pushing that button. Papa tells me that he has never had to push that button and doesn't intend to.

After the speech, Papa says he knows just the thing to help me get to know the crew better. He reaches for the speaker microphone and announces: "New pup is getting morning coffee. What do you want?"

I know I look unhappy, but I nod my OK to Papa.

The speaker comes to life: "Tea, double sugar."

"Black, two cups."

"Coffee, double, double."

"Coffee, double cream, single sugar."

"Coffee, cream and double sugar."

"Hot chocolate for me," Papa finishes.

I stand in front of the machine and shake my head because I just knew something like this was going to happen. I didn't pack a lunch because I was lazy. Instead, I brought four dollars to buy food from the vending machines. Now these cretins were going to be served coffee and tea by the guy who wouldn't be eating or drinking anything tonight.

It gets worse. Phase 1 of the new-guy orientation begins when I hand out the cups.

"Hey, I didn't order coffee double cream!"

"Yes, you did."

"No, I didn't. Are you calling me a liar?"

"No, but you said double cream and he wanted two cups of black!"

"There you go. Now I *know* you're full of shit because he never drinks black, do ya?"

"I'd sooner drink piss than black coffee."

That can be arranged, I think to myself. This crap continues all the way down the line until everyone has a chance to bitch about the order being wrong, or how the coffee is cold, or something else that the pup has messed up. This becomes a nightly ritual until the seventh and final midnight shift.

"Who needs coffee?" I ask reluctantly, knowing it was time for another round of "screw the new guy."

"Nothing for me, thanks," Papa says.

Huh? I'm sure I misunderstood him, but before I can ask, the rest of the crew chimes in over the speakers.

"None here."

"I'm fine."

"I'm good, thanks for asking though."

What the hell are these guys up to now? I know they're going to try to irritate the pup.

"Jesus Christ! Did I just call myself Pup?" I say out loud as I rub my forehead.

"Hey, Pup. We're all going over to Denny's after work to celebrate the end of midnights. I hope you can come," Papa says.

Instead of coffee, these sons a bitches think I'm going to buy them breakfast! Oh, I'll go! Just to tell each and every one of them to kiss my ass!

Slamming my car door shut, I storm to the Denny's entrance, hell-bent on giving every member of "D" crew a piece of my mind. In a room off to the side I see Papa and his assistant operator. I walk up to the chair closest to Papa Dunn, spin it around, and look directly at him.

"You know what I think, Papa?" I hiss.

"Yeah. That we're a bunch of assholes and you'd like to kick our asses," Papa says calmly. "Well, today you get even, Pup. You order anything you want and as much as you want because 'D' crew is buying."

Each guy comes to the table and either rubs my head or pats me on the back and welcomes me to the crew.

"I'm just the recorder, guys, I'm not really part of your crew," I say.

"Bullshit!" says Papa. "You record all the tons we run. Without you no one would ever know how great we are. Yep, from now on you're part of the 'D' crew 'til death do us part."

Over the next few months I get to know the guys better and why they got their nicknames. Don "Dozer" Reese has an amazing ability to fall asleep anytime, anywhere. It's true. If I told Dozer I had to go to the bathroom and that I'd be back in five minutes, he would spend one minute getting to sleep, three minutes sleeping, and one minute waking up to get ready for my return. Dozer sleeps before the start of the monthly safety meetings. When trains block the entrance to the mill, he sleeps. If I ever gave Dozer a ride anywhere, I could expect to talk to myself because he would be sleeping.

Dozer is what I call a mill zombie. That's an insane breed of worker who never refuses overtime. In fact, mill zombies would work a double every day if they could. Lack of sleep wears them down. Dozer, who is twenty-nine years old, actually looks like he's in his forties. Every mill zombie has a dream that drives him or her to work like a maniac. Dozer's dream is to retire at forty-five and move to Florida to enjoy his oceanfront property. We all give Dozer a hard time and tell him he's nuts.

Papa stops all the harassment when he says, "Every man needs his dreams and I think Dozer's is a fine dream to shoot for."

"Ah, why not?" Smurf Davis agrees. "He'll fit right in with all the retirees down there cause he's gonna look like he's sixty!"

We laugh until we see Papa looking over his safety glasses at us. Nothing more is ever said about Dozer's dream.

Smurf Davis works on the entry end with Dozer. He got his name from *The Smurfs* cartoon show because he's barely five feet tall. But you don't want to mess with him. He has forearms like Popeye and a big barrel chest. He combs his jet-black hair straight back like a greaser and wears a handlebar mustache. He's an avid outdoorsman—a real man's man. Oh yeah, and he's got the temper of an Irishman. If someone pokes fun at him or calls him a name, Smurf responds with a display of fists. He cocks his arms, nudges his nose with his right fist and says, "Sure'n, you'll be taking that back now." This is the offender's only chance to apologize before Smurf tears into him like a buzzsaw.

Then there's "Doc" Winters, the craneman. He got his nickname because his lunch box is a pharmacy of over-the-counter medications and— let's just say—"prescription" drugs. Doc always has a cure for what ails us, but we have to double check what he's dispensing because we might be better off with the illness. Doc will always be the stereotypical 60's hippie. He takes great pride in the fact that his articles have appeared in *High Times* magazine. He takes less pride in his hair, which I venture to say hasn't been cut in twenty years. It was probably the last time he washed it too. He wears it in two salt-and-pepper braids and sports a scraggly beard. The whiskers under the corners of his mouth have an orange tint from tobacco drool. He wears sunglasses day and night.

Marty Collins, our coiler, is a ball of nerves. Marty has no nickname because we're afraid to give him one. He would probably have an anxiety attack wondering why we chose a particular name. Marty eats constantly but gains no weight due to his constant fretting. He's convinced people are looking at the freckles on his face whenever anyone talks to him. He also thinks he's contracted every terminal disease in the book. Even though he has miraculously triumphed over every one of them, that doesn't stop him from looking in the mirror to see if the next big ailment is coming. Most of the crew would just as soon leave Marty out of things, but Papa is afraid we'll find him dangling from a rope with a note saying he was despondent over being excluded.

Finally, there's Lester Grimm, or "Chief." Lester is a heavy man with more hair in his ears than on his head. He has the biggest nose I've ever seen and cheeks that puff out like a jack-o-lantern. Lester was involved in a bad accident that injured his brain. It slowed his actions and his speech, but that doesn't bother Papa.

One day I'm in the office and I see Lester cornered in a room with a bunch of supervisors and stuffed shirts. I go back to the line and tell the guys it looks like Lester is getting the ax.

Papa is working alone because his assistant just retired and he's waiting for a new guy to bid on the job. He grabs the microphone and tells Marty to watch the line.

"Pup, show me where this meeting's at."

Papa barges right into the meeting room. "Sorry I'm late," he announces. "Where are we so far?"

The next fifteen minutes are a swearfest. The gist of it is that management wants Lester to retire because of his disability. Papa tells them that they can't take away a man's dignity like that without at least trying to help him. Papa, finally fed up, looks up at Lester and says, "Lester, can you blink your eyes fast?"

"Y . . .y . . . yes," Lester says.

"Fine. Lester, blink once if yes, twice if no, OK?"

Lester blinks once.

"Lester, do you want to retire?"

Blink! Blink!

"Lester, can you do most of the assistant operator's job?"

Blink!

"Lester, if trouble comes up, can you duck quick and get out of trouble if you have to?"

Blink!

"Good enough for me," Papa says. "He's got the years. I've got the opening. I'll take him."

"You don't know what you're saying," one of the supervisors says. "He can't do the work and he's a safety liability."

"The only thing you guys want is prime tons of steel, and I'll give them to you like I always do—with Lester's help," Papa says. "Leave the problems to me and if it don't work out then we can talk about this shit."

The men gathered at the table sort of look at each other for someone to refute Papa's demands. No one does.

"That's settled. Lester, go get your work clothes on. We're working today."

I sneak a quick peak at Lester. Tears are pouring down his cheeks. I wish I hadn't looked. Now I'm fighting back tears.

As it turns out, Papa will have to do his job plus about sixty percent of Lester's job from now on. He'll do it for five years until Lester finally retires on his own terms with a full pension. Papa never complains once.

"Gentlemen, Lester Grimm will be joining our crew today as my new assistant," Papa announces over the speaker when we get back to the workstation.

"Works for me, Papa," Dozer says.

"I reckon I'll back my captain's decision," Doc says.

"Full steam ahead," Smurf shouts.

"F . . . fine with me, Papa," Marty squeaks. "Did I write the stuff down OK in there while you were gone?"

"Yes, Marty. Everything looks fine. Thanks for filling in for me."

A few minutes later our supervisor, Buck Timmons, hits the airwaves. "All right, Papa, you win," he says sarcastically. "Lester is all yours and believe me, I'm glad I'm not in your shoes."

Buck is whatever the current management wants him to be. He has worked with us as a friend and as a foe. This year, management has him in the role of adversary. Buck's waist measurement probably exceeds his height. He has five chins and wheezes when he talks. He'll eat anything. I've seen him chuck things down that would make a billy goat puke.

"Well, we're even then," Papa tells Buck, "I'm glad I don't fit into your pants."

"Hey, Buck!" Smurf yells, "I hear Circus World is having a close-out sale on tents this weekend!"

We wait for a comeback, but Buck doesn't respond. We win that round, but Buck will make life a living hell for us for a while to get even.

"You did good, Papa," Dozer shouts.

"Good has nothing to do with it," Papa says. "It was just the right thing to do."

Autumn arrives bringing much-desired cooler temperatures. It also brings my twenty-first birthday. Lucky me. I'm working four to twelve tonight. I won't even be able to celebrate with my family until this weekend.

I reach my desk to start the shift.

"Hello there, birthday boy," I hear Smurf say on the speaker. "Have we got a surprise for you!"

Boy, I'll say, how did they find out it's my birthday? I didn't tell anyone.

I join the crew in the operator's shack. There's a little white cake with a big twenty-one candle in the center. They sing a horrible rendition of "Happy Birthday."

"Thanks, guys. What a nice surprise," I say.

"This? Oh, this ain't shit compared to what we have planned for you," Smurf says grinning. "You're gonna get introduced to a little establishment known as The Scuttlebutt, Pup, me lad. Has my new lady got a night planned for you!"

He runs off to thread up a new coil. Once he clears the door, I spin around and say, "What the hell is The Scuttlebutt?"

My excited comrades tell me it's a sleazy strip joint. Smurf, who's a regular, has met a dancer there he hopes to make his fifth wife. He's so proud of her talents that he wants to show her off to us. They tell me her act climaxes with her incredible ability to pick up quarters with her . . . well, let's just say she doesn't use her mouth or hands. Smurf, who's ordinarily jealous as hell, feels it would be wrong to deny his friends the chance to witness her extraordinary skills.

"Is it just me, or does anyone else find this demented?" I ask.

"You don't want to hurt Smurf's feelings, do ya?" Dozer asks.

I figure I'm being played for a fool. I look to Papa who will usually give me a look to let me know if something is on the level or not. To my horror, he shrugs his shoulders and says, "Happy Birthday, Pup."

That night I'm frozen in disbelief at what I'm witnessing.

"Way to go, baby! Woo WOO! Great set, honey!" Smurf yells. He applauds wildly and then elbows me in the arm. "Isn't she something?"

After she freshens up, or whatever strippers do, Smurf's girl comes to our table. Even though she wants to sit with us, we have to continue to buy her rum and cokes so she can stay there.

"Hi, birthday boy," she says extending her hand. "Here's a little keepsake for you."

It's a quarter.

"Gosh, uh, thanks . . . I'm sorry, I don't know your name."

"It's Naughty Nina," she giggles.

Before I can say anything else, a large black woman weighing at least 230 pounds sidles up next to me.

Oh God, please let me wake up from this nightmare.

"I hear someone is having a birthday today," she says, nimbly throwing a leg over my thighs to straddle me.

The guys cheer and give me the thumbs up sign. She looks into my eyes and smiles while reaching into her mouth. She pulls out her dentures, leans in close and whispers with rummy breath, "Have you ever had a gum job?"

Fate saves me from certain humiliation when a shouting match erupts behind us. A man is trying to leave the club with a can of beer. I don't know if it's the house rules or the law, but the bouncer won't let the man take the beer outside. The tension escalates and the bouncer finally pulls a gun from under his coat and points it at the man. Strippers are screaming and running for the back room. My birthday girl jumps off me and joins the exodus, restoring the blood flow to my numb thighs. I stand up to get a better look.

"Shoot the bastard!" someone yells.

"I'll do it. I'll shoot you dead," the bouncer screams.

The drunk inches closer to the door.

I can't believe this guy's going to get shot over a beer! I edge closer to the drunk. Impulsively, I fish two dollars out of my pocket and thrust them at him.

"Dude, take this! There's a liquor store down the road."

"Get outta my way!" the bouncer shouts.

The drunk calls me something, but he's too drunk to be understood.

"Please, dude!" I plead with him. "You don't want your wife and kids to hear that you were killed over a beer in front of a strip joint, do you? For God's sake, give the bouncer the beer and take this money. There's a liquor store two miles down the road."

The drunk, eyes unfocused, stands there swaying for an eternity. "Take your damn beer," he says shoving the can into my chest. He stumbles out the door.

The incident leaves me stone-cold sober. I turn to Dozer and tell him I'm going home. As we walk to our cars I feel an arm drape across my shoulders. It's Papa.

"Quite a night, eh, Papa?" I say meekly.

"Pup, that was the stupidest thing I've ever seen anyone do. Remind me to never drink with you again," he says patting me on the back. He turns and heads for his car.

"Hey, Psycho, here's that black chick's number in case you're still horny," Smurf says.

"My wife loves this first snowfall crap," Dozer says as we watch giant flakes fall outside the warehouse door. It's been a rather uneventful few months, but now we're heavy into the Christmas spirit planning our party.

We see Bob Bailey coming toward us.

"Grab your ankles, boys." Dozer says. "Booze Bailey is coming down and it looks like he wants to hump some hiney!"

"Aw, shit!" Marty says. "I don't need this."

Bailey is the chief inspector. He rides around in his golf cart checking for defects like wavy edges or poor coating on the metal. He also likes to piss people off. I felt sorry for him once because I thought he was crippled. He never leaves the golf cart he rides in. He just pulls up to the inspection table, looks over the samples, and drives away. Later, I found out he's an alcoholic and drives everywhere so people can't see him stagger when he walks.

Doc calls him "mood nose." Remember mood rings? Doc says Bailey's perpetually red nose changes color when he gets angry. First it gets redder, then purple, and finally it turns a dark blue-green. Once Doc put a Quaalude in Bailey's coffee and it took ten hours before we could wake him up.

I see Bailey coming down the aisle in his cart. Smurf is running fast behind him. I know the Christmas elves are up to no good. Bailey pulls up his cart. He looks like Rudolph. He wanders into the back offices to talk with the line inspectors.

Smurf quickly grabs the bander and disconnects the air-pressure hose from it. He connects an impact wrench to the hose and takes the lug nuts off the golf cart's back tires in seconds. He's faster than an Indy pit crew. He returns the hose and races back down the line.

I love every minute of this and can't wait for Bailey to return. Marty paces back and forth nervously, convinced he'll be implicated somehow.

"It's moments like this that make life worth living," Doc says over the intercom.

Bailey finally reappears. He walks over to the intercom and says, "Papa, keep your eyes open. You're dangerously close to running shit here."

"Thanks for your inspirational speech, Bob, and have a nice drink—I mean day," Papa says.

Bailey gingerly walks over to his cart, climbs in, and speeds away. About thirty feet later both back wheels come off. I laugh myself into a coughing spasm. Even Marty can't help but laugh.

Bailey turns bright red with anger. He grabs the two tires and slams them onto the cart. He has a sinister look on his face and would love to nail us for good. But what can he do? He knows he's violating mill policy by drinking on the job. If he squeals on us, he's just begging for trouble. He calls for someone to come pick him up and we turn our attention back to the job.

Spring arrives and the world is in bloom. The day I thought would never come is here. Papa is retiring today. His back has been ailing him and he has decided to take it easy at home. He gets a lot of gifts and everyone tells their favorite stories. I feel terrible. I just can't imagine working without him leading us—pushing us—saying things like, "Can you handle it or am I going to have to push the button?"

I already miss my mentor.

With the glue gone, the team falls apart quickly. Dozer and Smurf fight constantly. It gets so bad that Smurf takes a job working for another line at the north end of the plant to get away. Doc says the line has bad karma and puts in for a transfer. Marty says he can't take the stress of the job and gets a job driving a tractor. I take a job in the stores department. It's like the mill's hardware store. I don't see the rest of the crew for months.

Papa didn't tell us the real reason he retired. I don't find out until Dozer calls me on a hot and steamy July afternoon to tell me Papa is dead.

When his back had started troubling him, Papa sought medical advice. The doctors suggested exploratory surgery. Papa took vacation time for the procedure so we wouldn't find out about it. The surgeons discovered he was full of cancer, immediately closed him up, and suggested that he get his affairs in order because he didn't have long to live. We never even knew he was sick. He always sounded happy when I called him on the phone.

Today is Papa's funeral. I arrive at the funeral parlor five minutes early. Strange. Everyone from the crew pulls up at the same time.

We got to the job on time, Papa.

We all embrace and poke fun at how rigid and uncomfortable we look in suits that we obviously just purchased. It starts to drizzle, so we go inside.

We all go over to Papa's wife and hug her and tell her how sorry we are. We mill around for a few minutes until we can't justify not going to the coffin any longer. We walk up together and look at our leader.

The cancer has taken its toll. He looks pale and weak. His skin droops from his face like his skin is two sizes too big. I'm the first to lose it, but the others aren't far behind.

We sit through the ceremony, but I don't hear a word of the funeral. I just keep thinking of Papa. After the service, Dozer goes to talk to Papa's wife.

He walks back and says, "When they're ready to close the casket, she said we can do it."

Finally, when it's just Papa's wife and children, we stand alongside the casket. Dozer reaches into his pocket and produces the big red emergency button. He slips it under Papa's crossed hands.

"Now no one will ever be able to push the button, Papa," Smurf says, his voice cracking.

Bawling like babies, we turn and walk into the next room. It isn't long until Papa's casket is carried past us.

The weather is miserable as we drive to the cemetery. The wind is howling and rain is coming down in buckets. The funeral party is reduced to just the widow and her children, plus five men standing in a row. The rain beats our faces and our suits are soaked and heavy, but no one moves a muscle.

No weather is going to stop us from showing respect for the greatest man we ever met.

Back at Papa's house, his children tell us they're overwhelmed by the number of people who came to say goodbye to their father.

"Did you ever know what your father did at the mill?" I ask.

"No, just that he ran some line thingy," the oldest daughter says.

For the next four hours we bring their father, the Steelworker, back to life for them. We tell our tales from the days when we were "D" crew.

We leave the house and return to our cars. Smurf beckons us to his truck. He opens a cooler and hands everyone a beer.

"Here's to Papa, the best damn operator in the whole steel industry!" he says. We slug down a few swallows.

We begin apologizing to each other for fighting, for leaving the group and for giving up on each other.

We are silent for a minute. Then, without saying anything, we instinctively bring our beers together for a toast.

"We promise to never speak ill of others, Papa," I say.

"We will get together around the holidays to celebrate the good times we had," Dozer says.

"Long live 'D' crew!" Smurf shouts.

"To 'D' crew!" we say in unison. We all take a drink.

Doc hoists up his can and says, "And God bless us, every one!"

We look at each other and burst out laughing. Each of us grabs another beer from the cooler and starts shaking the cans and spraying them as we chase each other around the yard. Maybe it's not the best tribute for a fallen comrade, but Papa never cared what we did or said as long as we showed up on time and did the job right. Somehow it just feels right.

"See ya later, Papa," I say, then I yell at the sky: "Hey, angels, new meat's coming up!"

Deliverance

Wendy Marciniak

He's home.
I hear the hum
of the garage door.
Soon I will see him trudge in,
and in a look,
I will know
what the night has dealt.

He will sit.
I will sort
through the brown paper bag,
worn soft as doeskin,
for the tightly rolled work clothes
and the thermos with its
tepid, tired, last drops
that smelled so good when it left here.

Greasy sandwich bags, potato chip crumbs,
a squashed cookie
all wear the same
metallic scent of the work.

Those things I can count on—
sometimes more.
The occasional paperback, odd tool,
cigarettes and Tylenol.
What you need
to survive the night
in the place that never sleeps.

I throw out the used.
Tomorrow, in the light of afternoon,
I'll replenish what I can.

He will take it,
and I will think of him
with his coffee, his book,
his Tylenol dessert.

I will hear the hum again
and be ready for the handoff.

My midnight date
with whatever is left.

SECTION V: The Cost of Steel

Rolling Along the Line

Marty Marciniak

Like the blooms, ingots, slabs and shapes that spewed from the furnaces, converters, and open hearths, the USWA was further refined into an organization that improved the lives of its members in the workplace and beyond.

Basic labor agreements that steadily increased wages, benefits packages, and fair treatment of workers brought an unprecedented standard of living for blue-collar workers and their families.

An unwritten "Social Compact" between business, labor, and the government prevented the typical post-war recurrence of a depressed economy as increased labor costs were easily offset by improved rates of productivity and the economic and social stability brought about by "labor peace." All parties held a stake in the Marshall Plan's success in rebuilding war-torn Europe and Japan.

As a union "conceived in conflict and baptized in blood," the USWA could still, however, take to the streets and bring the line to a screeching halt, as it was forced to do for 116 days in 1959 to protect Steelworkers from attempted violations of their hard-won rights.

Through the '60s and into the '70s, the line continued to roll, but the corporate myopia and lethargy that gradually crept into the domestic steel industry led to steadily increasing productions costs—even as the immutable laws of supply and demand teetered out of balance.

Obsolete technologies in the mill were blindly and stubbornly maintained despite the availability of improved processes and products, setting the stage for a disastrous downturn for the domestic steel industry as a whole, and for the USWA in particular.

Snow Danced in August

Joe E. Gutierrez

On any given morning, blessed with a cloudless, sun-driven sky, we enjoyed a marvelous sight of sparkling silver dust, floating down ever so gently; dancing a Beethoven waltz—one-two-three, one-two-three—in and out of a beam of sunlight that cut through a sliver of corrugated wall high above our turned-up heads—delirious with the beauty of it all.

We were forever anxious for this delightful diversion of falling fireflies that took our minds off the monotony of a monotonous job.

We worked in a giant building that housed four galvanize lines. The lines spewed out tons and tons of galvanize steel, coated with melted zinc, used to make automobile bodies and mufflers for those automobiles and pots and pans and everything nice. Hundreds of workers manned and maintained a continuous process that made this all possible. Let me tell you about those workers and that process.

Each galvanize line has a gas furnace approximately the length of a city block through which a strip of steel is run. The furnace is heated to over 1800 degrees to burn impurities off the steel as it moves through the furnace. When the steel strip exits the furnace, it immediately runs through an enclosed steel box that extends into a ten-foot-square iron pot containing molten zinc. As the heated strip of steel exits the pot, it is coated with the hot zinc. The strip then runs up into a cooling tower which is approximately 100 feet from the floor. At the mouth of this cooling tower is a padded turn-down roll six feet wide that turns as long as the strip is moving. The strip runs over this roll into a stretch of housing that contains fans that quickly cool the strip down. When the strip leaves the cooling tower, it proceeds down to the basement through what is called a loop car. The coated strip eventually finds its way to the receiving section where it is wound into a steel coil and shipped to a satisfied customer.

This was Plant No.1, Galvanize Department, Inland Steel. I am everyone who worked there or visited there and partook of that wondrous sight of dancing silver dust. I am Union and I am Management. I'm the customer who visited the plant and inspected the product. I'm the teacher who organized a trip to the steel mill, and I'm the school-kid visitor who stared in awe at the monster machines and burning hot steel. I am the wife of my husband who worked there and I am the husband of my wife who also worked there. I am the mayor of this fine city, and I am the councilman, and I am a member of the entourage that toured this fine Galvanize Department with silver dust falling from the sky.

Many times over the years, we visited this site. Usually it was in the summer, when the company allowed visitors to visit, and other times too. There was never a time though, up until the middle of the memorable 1980s, that the sparkling spectacle did not occur. We just couldn't see it until that beam of sunlight shined through the cracks in the west wall. When that happened, it was a miracle that removed the dark filter from our eyes and we beheld an existing, continuous panorama of beauty that was hidden in the darkness. It was an August snowfall of silver flakes captured in sunlight.

Our eyes immediately became microscopes allowing us to see those spinning half circles that whirled madly in place all the time, hidden. It became so fascinating that we prayed for sunshine and that welcome beam of light. We fought to work in that section! "Let me work there! No, let me work there!" We were all hungry for that little bit of magic.

Eventually, we all had our turn. We all worked there year after year after year, and after awhile, we no longer clamored for that spot. I guess we got tired. It was no longer new. The mystique was gone, but we did enjoy when someone new came to work. We watched their face light up the first time they saw it. They always turned to us, the old-timers, and said, "Hey, is that pretty! Do you see that?" And nonchalantly, we would say, "Aw, that's nothin'. It's always there . . . you just can't see it all the time."

Where did that magic come from and why was it there? Let me explain. Remember that padded roll up at the mouth of the cooling tower? Well, it had to be replaced once every one and a half or two weeks, sometimes more often, depending on how fast they ran the line and how quickly the roll snowflaked away. There were four galvanize lines, so that means there were four of these padded rolls. When they were initially installed, they were probably as tall in circumference as they were wide and they were six feet wide. As the exceedingly hot strip ran over and around the padded row, the roll began to break apart—a dancing, glittering silver sliver at a time—and that's when the sky came alive.

It's been a few years now since new technology stepped in and kind of took over the Galvanize Department. There were four galvanize lines. Now there are two. The building where number one and two lines stood, now stands empty and desolate. The lines were torn down leaving nothing but a skeleton of rusting steel girders a city block long. There are no lights, or very few. I've gone back there a few times and walked through that graveyard remembering, thinking about the good times and the bad, and if I try really hard, I can still see the strip flying by and hear the whooosshhh of the gas lighting in the furnace and the foreman yelling, "Let's go! Let's get this line running!" Yeah, I can still hear him yelling and we did what we had to do.

About a year before they decided to shut the lines down, we discovered that the dancing, one-two-three, one-two-three, silver dust was "ASBESTOS." Our union had to fight like hell to get the company to stop using those damn padded rolls. We know now the danger that product has produced.

Most everybody that worked in the Galvanize Department a few years has tested positive. When that pretty stuff was falling, it didn't care if you were company or union. Everybody breathed it. Who am I? I'm everybody. Can't walk too far now. I get tired real fast and it hurts when I breathe, sometimes. And to think, we used to fight over that job.

"ASBESTOS." Ain't nothin' now but a word.

Leftovers

Chuck Canty

A fierce storm blanketed Northwest Indiana with a half-foot of snow. Looking out the window the next morning, I knew I was going to have a hell of a time getting to the mill, so I decided to leave early.

The snow was still falling and—as usual—the snowplows hadn't hit the road yet. The drive to work, usually a quick 30-minute trip, took an hour-and-a-half as I wrestled to keep my car on the road.

Another four inches had fallen in the time it took to get to the mill. I was 10 minutes late and the asshole supervisor, Vinny, told me he was going to have to dock me two-tenths of an hour. My co-worker, Andy Stanford, was right behind me, and Vinny said he was getting docked, too. We were assigned to work on the snowplows so we grabbed our tools and got started.

An hour later, I realized we were the only mechanics in the shop. I thought most of the crew was out hooking up salt spreaders or driving tow trucks, but it turned out the entire crew had called it off because of the storm. This really pissed me off. I'd made the effort to get to work in a blizzard and that stinking supervisor, Vinny, was going to dock me for being 10 minutes late! Ain't no fucking way!

The assistant-general foreman came over to where Andy and I were working and asked how long the repairs were going to take. I told him, then decided to get this docking issue settled. He listened to my beef, stood there thinking a minute, and walked back to his office. A few minutes later, Vinny walked up and told Andy and me that he had reconsidered and wasn't going to dock us. He acted like it was his idea, but we knew the assistant-general foreman had talked to him.

Half an hour later, Vinny sent me out to tow a truck that was stuck near the oxygen furnace and blocking the railroad tracks. The snow was still coming down and piling up against the building in four-foot drifts.

I drove the tow truck to the oxygen furnace. The stupid-ass driver had made a U-turn in the middle of a rail crossing and had gotten a six-wheel dump truck with a snowplow and salt spreader hung up on a rail switch. There were two locomotives waiting for the crossing to be cleared. It took me more than an hour to get the truck freed and off the tracks.

By the time I got back to the garage, I was a popsicle. The supervisor asked Andy and me to pull a double shift. Andy was concerned. He said he'd gotten stranded in the mill for three days during a snowstorm in 1968 and didn't want to go through that again. I told him if we doubled over, there would be less traffic and we stood a better chance of making it home. He agreed and we kept working on the plows.

At the start of the three o'clock shift, we found out the second crew of mechanics had called off work because of the weather. I tried to call my wife Debbie to tell her I was working overtime, but the lines were down. John Fletcher, the general foreman, came into the office as I was trying to call her and asked why I'd been using the phone so much. I told him that I was trying to call my wife. He told me to get the hell out of the office.

Wow, that's real gratitude, I thought.

At 6 p.m., it was time to take a dinner break. I hadn't brought enough food with me for a double shift, so I turned to the vending machines. But because of the storm, the vending company never showed up to restock the machines and they were all empty.

Andy and I sat down in the lunchroom and talked to kill the lunch hour. We were arguing about who makes the best pizza in town when I noticed a guy carrying a large platter of sandwiches, soft drinks, potato chips and other snacks into the office where the supervisors were sitting. A few minutes later, more supervisors showed up and they had themselves a real party going on in there.

"Think they'll ask us to join them?" Andy said.

"I don't know, but I'm going to find out," I said. "I'm going to pretend to make a phone call. Maybe that'll remind them that we're starving out here."

I walked into the office and picked up the phone, but the line was still out.

"I told you to quit coming in here to use the phone," Fletcher barked when he saw me. "Use the payphone outside!"

So that was it. We were union people—good enough to fix their broken equipment but not good enough to eat with salaried employees.

We went back to work. Two hours later, Vinny finally came over and offered what was left of the food. All that was left was a couple of bags of chips.

"They left us the scraps," I told Andy. "Fuck this shit. I'm not working another minute of overtime when this shift is over."

It took me two hours to get home. I had to park at the end of my street and walk home because of the snow. I didn't feel guilty when I took the next three days off while the plows cleared the roads. That was the last time I ever stayed over due to a crisis situation. Now I know why the other mechanics made no attempt to get to work in the blizzard.

Don't Mind the Noise

J.A. Orellana

It's just the grumbling in my brain
Incessant ramblings screaming to get out—
break free from the squirrel cage that holds
the endless clanging of drunken thoughts.
Banging
Banging against the steel bars
    Like empty tin cups protesting the confined pickled
conditions:
    Death row inside the steel-hard ivory cranium scattered with
    shredded tripe's flayed thoughts.
Please oh please
    Don't mind the mindless banging
    clanging against the steel bars.

Women in the Mill

Jennifer Jones

From the first day women start working in the mill, they hear things like, "You don't belong here," or, "You're taking a job from a man." I've heard people say, "You can't pull your own weight, so just leave." I doubt a day passes when a woman somewhere in the mill doesn't hear one of these phrases.

I've been in the mill for almost thirty years and I know words can hurt—especially when I've gone out of my way to carry the biggest load, or do the biggest part of a job or not ask for help when I needed it. I know it's been a lot easier for me than for the women who preceded me. I can only imagine the abuse they suffered through just trying to support their families.

Some days I get angry at the callous remarks and think *I'm not going to take this anymore*! But I think of the women who came before me and my anger vaporizes. I appreciate the path they carved for me and others who followed. I admire their willingness to keep going and not quit. I applaud their fortitude and courage. I cherish their spirit and sense of adventure. And as I walk in their footsteps, I hope that one day my actions will benefit others. I thank them for just being who they were and allowing me to be who I am. I thank them from the bottom of my heart. May there be women in the mill as long as there is a mill.

The Union's Best Friend

Joe Lunchbox

If you dial 1-800-BASTARD you'll hear my pal Charlie's voice say "hello" on the first ring. Punch up a word search for "scum bag" on the Internet and his picture will pop onto your screen.

Charlie is probably the most dangerous type of manager ever to crawl out from under a rock. He pretends to be your best buddy and that he's genuinely concerned about your problems. He'll look you straight in the eye, nod, smile, and pat you on the back while his mind races to figure out a way to screw you someday. When he asks about the wife and kids, a part of him will secretly be disappointed to hear you say, "They're fine. Doing great."

That's the bad news about my pal, Charlie. The good news is that, in the long run, Charlie always loses. He loses because he beats himself.

Charlie flat-out hates the union. Even after Charlie reaches an agreement with the union about a work rule or crew size, he'll usually try his level-best to undermine the intent of that agreement, usually through confidential, but stern directives telling his underling supervisors to ignore the agreement. Charlie covers his tracks pretty well. It's the other supervisors who get left holding the bag. After this happens a few times, his subordinates get to despising him even more than the union does. They get their revenge by subtly and passively providing the union with just enough inside information to let the union come out on top in the end. Although they've got to maintain the illusion of doing exactly what Charlie says, they'd really rather see the bastard lose.

So, I'm not being facetious when I call Charlie my "pal." He's such a world-class bastard to both sides of the fence, that in his own bassackward way he's probably one of the best friends the union has. Even when he's not trying to make himself look good by making the other managers look bad, he still does the union plenty of good by picking unnecessary fights with the union. One of the inherent threats to large local unions is apathy. Nothing builds immediate solidarity among workers like a full frontal assault from management. Thanks, Charlie. It's worth saying again—managers like Charlie are the union's best friends.

Someday my pal Charlie may be strolling the seashore at low tide. He might just stumble across the fabled Aladdin's lamp. Chances are he'll pick it up, rub it, and release the genie who'll grant him the customary three wishes. Charlie will review his options. World peace? Health and happiness for himself and family? Eternal life? Fabulous wealth? Nah, Charlie will follow his heart. Wish No. 1: Bust the union. Wish No. 2: Bust the union. Wish No. 3: Bust the union. The genie, who has lived for thousands of years and has seen it all many times over, will think to himself, *Geez, what a bastard!*

Dear Lisa

Norman J. Brown, Jr.

What did you come here to see?

Men wearing dirty clothes—unlearned and unable to hold intelligent conversation?

What do you think a Steelworker is supposed to be like?

Am I not the epitome of intelligence?

Yet, you expected one with little or no ability to form meaningful, deep thoughts into sentences?

I am the new breed of Steelworker.

I may see myself as more than that, but I am also able to see myself as a part of this group . . .

of guys who sweat night and day, sometimes working sixteen hours straight, all so they can . . .

support their families, pay their bills, and supply you, the consumer, with a product that is . . .

useful for everyday life.

Without me, you may not see a can of soup.

You may not even drive the car you drive.

So believe me when I say that you would feel the effects if I stopped doing what I do.

So don't judge me by the title Steelworker.

I am a high-tech individual who makes up a new work force on the rise—a new guard that will revolutionize steelmaking. I am part of a new culture that is growing in numbers. If you are open-minded, let me bless your world with many ideas you will never hear outside these walls, and maybe never care to contemplate. For I am in a place where many have died, including my grandfather. In essence, he gave his life for you, as have many others. But many know not of the sacrifices made by people like my grandfather.

I ask that you open your closed mind so I can put something in there that's real, and erase the imaginary world you have already designed in your psyche. Give me one chance and I can show you a world filled with characters that could be on TV.

Characters who need no lines.

Characters that will make you laugh, cry and even angry.

But there's only one catch: they are real people, not characters on TV. These are real people with real lives who are filled with dreams and ideas just as you. You would think that some could change the world. Others you would think would make this world a living hell.

So I ask once again, take a look at these people and tell me what you see, not what you imagine. These are Steelworkers, yes, but real people first.

Some are educated, some not.

Some are likeable, some aren't.

You must see for yourself and discover those hidden treasures beneath the dirt and the grease they wear as a garment and you will find artists, writers, carpenters and architects. All like you, but active in a different part of society.

Just take a look and you will see.

SECTION VI: The Finishing End

Cobbled and Hobbled

Marty Marciniak

A ribbon of steel zips along, through pickling, annealing, sizing, coating and other operations . . . increasing its cost—and likewise its value—through each progressive step. Gauged, sampled, tested and recorded, the final legs of its journey are perhaps the most crucial. But the low-pitched rumble of a rapidly accelerating oscillation of the strip provides scant warning—even to the seasoned ear—of the crash that will inevitably follow within seconds . . .

The stunning announcements of plant closings and discontinued product lines sent shockwaves through communities that reverberated to their roots. Once-mighty mill towns became ghost towns, seemingly overnight, as 400,000 Steelworkers' livelihoods disappeared in just two short years. The USWA's membership dropped from 1.1 million in 1981 to 710,000 in 1983. By 1993, the USWA claimed only 540,000 dues-paying members, less than half of the 1.4 million peak in 1979. But stark numbers alone only tell part of the story.

Miles of smokestacked buildings, providing thousands of bill-paying, mortgage-paying, tax-paying jobs, vanished under the wrecking ball and bulldozer. What had taken decades to build was destroyed in a matter of months. The security, dependability and dignity of jobs in the mill was suddenly gone.

With each successive wave of shutdowns and layoffs from the late '70s through the '80s, state unemployment compensation and severance checks were like band-aids on bullet wounds. The bleeding just wouldn't stop, and the golden parachutes provided to outgoing corporate executives only rubbed salt deep into those wounds.

Down, but certainly not out, the USWA rebounded to 700,000 members by the century's end. Learning important lessons from its past, the USWA rebuilt itself on firm foundations of strong pattern contracts, membership education, renewed organizing strategies, and aggressive political action. As the scars of the old wounds slowly heal, they serve as a grim reminder to never again allow the poor maintenance procedures and obsolete business practices of employers to do so much damage to so many working people in so short a time.

Little Joe

Joe E. Gutierrez

Little Joe cautiously prepared to step down the newly painted, wheelchair-accessible yellow curb and glanced up and down the busy boulevard with the unease of an old man unsure of his balance. Looking up, he saw that the stop and go lights weren't working again. He carefully maneuvered his hand-carved, ivory-handled, ebony cane from his left hand to his right. Then he began to smile. Whenever he used his favorite walking stick for something other than walking, he would find himself daydreaming.

He could still hear her voice.

"That's genuine whale tooth, Mac," the old Maxwell Street bitch whistled to him through her two remaining teeth. He had bought it from her some forty years ago for a hard thirty-three dollars and fifty-five cents. The beer-breath broad wouldn't budge a penny. In fact, she threatened to raise the price the more he bickered. When he asked her if she could go lower, she squatted down and in a deep voice growled, "Thirty-three dollars and fifty-five cents." He never thought he would need it. He just liked it, especially the twenty-two inch razor-sharp sword that was hidden in the shaft. He never knew it was there, until Jessica, his granddaughter, who was using his cane for Tinker Bell's magic wand, found it while she was battling Captain Hook. It scared her when the blade fell out of the shaft because she thought she had broken it. She was only seven years old at the time. Made him promise that one day it would be hers.

He shook his head back to the present and with gnarled effort lifted his cane to the button that activated the "walk" signal. He knew it wouldn't work, but he pushed it anyway. Nothing happened. "Damn," he mumbled. "Nothing works!"

Overloaded semis and tanker trucks took advantage of the spent lights and sped through the intersection, leaving behind their diesel-smelling black exhaust that hid the street sign on the corner of Chicago Avenue and Indianapolis Boulevard.

Little Joe, that's what everyone called him, put in forty-four years at the steel mill before he decided to retire. Said he just couldn't handle the shit anymore. Besides, his bones were aching. Didn't move like he used to, but still got around. "You lost too much weight too soon, Lil' Joe," his buddy the "Doc" (who wasn't really a Doc, but wanted to be) told him. After Little Joe's wife died, he just didn't care to eat. Took a long time to get over it. They were together for forty-some years. He always thought that he would go first, but it didn't work out that way. One early Saturday in November she woke up coughing. Said she didn't feel well. He went to get her a glass of water, and by the time he came back, she was dead. Didn't even get a chance to say, "Goodbye, baby, I love you."

Dying is tough for the living. Been years since he buried her. For a long time, he woke himself up calling her name, dreaming she was cradled under his arm. Time's a great healer, if you let it. For the first few years her picture was in every room. Once he realized the pain and the pictures were synonymous, he took them down. When the kids came to the house, they put them back up. They just didn't know the hurt, but that's all right, they meant well.

He woke up at five every morning as if he were working the day shift. He dressed and walked to St. Mary's for early Mass, just as he did when he was a kid. Sometimes, when he was up to it, he climbed the circular staircase to the choir loft, found a chair next to the Hammond Organ and closed his eyes pretending to be twelve again, serving Mass for Monsignor Shea. If he concentrated hard enough, he could see his parents sitting in the front pew with his mother slowly fingering her Rosary beads. His mother never tired of telling him that she and Our Blessed Mother were on a first name basis. He never saw his father pray the Rosary, but when his father prayed, he prayed hard, just the way he did everything. For years they attended 5:30 a.m. Mass on Sunday. Then one day the Ol' Man just quit going. Said he'd prayed enough.

Damn Army Doctors! Little Joe thought as he stood waiting for the traffic to subside. *That son of a bitch shot me up with so much cortisone, I can still feel the needle pushing into my knee.*

"I'd like to push a needle up his ass," he grumbled to himself.

He carefully placed one foot in front of the other then abruptly stopped. The traffic lights on all four corners suddenly lit up, dancing from green to yellow to red, flashing a coded message to the speeding traffic with no response. He snarled out a curt "Damn!" to nobody in particular, and to everyone at once, especially the nameless faces behind the steering wheels and tinted glass windows of the nameless cars that rushed past him. Used to be able to look at a car a block away and tell if it was a Chevy, Ford, or Buick. No more.

"Damn traffic! Slow Down!" he shouted, knowing that he would be driving just as fast if he were on his way to work. No one seemed to smile at that time of day, whether they were coming or going from work. Mill traffic. Nothing changes except the faces.

It was the second week in July and it was already muggy at 5:20 in the morning. It hadn't rained for weeks. Little Joe stared at the flashing lights and was carried back to June of 1959. He was standing in almost the same spot in front of the Indiana Diner waiting for the bus to carry him to Inland Steel. He could still smell the diesel fumes as the bus pulled up and he could hear its air-controlled doors abruptly swing out their invitation for him to step in.

When he dropped the 15 cents in the slot, he knew he had one U.S. dollar to last him until he got on his feet. He was eighteen years old and he was broke. He thought the bus driver nodded hello. He wasn't sure, but he hoped so. Most of them were friendly, and when they acknowledged you, it made your day. The "horse bettors" would pay the fare just to get a nod or a friendly sideways glance. They all said it was lucky. If there was a connection, eye-to-eye, it was good. He would get off at the next stop and head for the bookie joint or the track. If the bus driver didn't look his way, he would ride on that bus, until he did. Little Joe never believed in that shit, but he wasn't taking any chances, especially then, because he needed a job.

Bus drivers were important people, because they got people where they needed to go, and in those days, everybody caught a bus. If you wanted to run away, you caught a bus. If you wanted to go back home, you caught a bus. If you were going on a date, you caught the bus together. Until you got some paychecks under your belt and you could afford to buy a car, you caught the bus. That bus driver was an important guy in everybody's life, and he was getting Little Joe to the Inland Employment Office by 8 a.m.

The bus was hardly ever full at this time of the morning. The factory workers were always up before the sun cracked the sky, and they were already pouring steel and stacking coils. But today was different. It seemed as if everyone was going to a steel employment office somewhere. Either Youngstown, Inland Steel, or General American. The mills were looking for bodies, and everybody on that bus was looking for work. Today there was only standing room. Any other time, women crammed the aisle carrying shopping bags from Goldblatt's or Penny's. Expectant mothers never had to stand very long. There was always a seat for them. Even the older women gave up their spots and gave them a knowing wink, as if to say, "I know what you are going through, honey." Kids going to and from school were a pain, but even they would give up a seat for a pregnant woman or an older person. The first time a kid gave Little Joe his seat was as traumatic as the first time some young kid called him mister. He felt like saying the proverbial, "Get away, kid, you bother me!"

Armed with his diploma and a letter of recommendation from Monsignor Shea, Little Joe took his place in line with the 180 soon-to-be Steelworkers. Little did he know that without that letter he would have been working in the blast furnace, breathing and sweating red dust, or in the Yard Department laying track, pounding spikes and spreading white gravel with all his other Latin brothers.

When he finally reached the head of the line, the man took the letter and looked him up and down and said, "Follow me." They walked away from the crowd and Mr. Johnson whispered to him that he was going to a nice department, No. 3 Cold Strip. Little Joe didn't know the difference between a "nice" department and a "bad" department. He just wanted to work. He went to St. Mary's that night and thanked Monsignor Shea for his help. The 82-year-old priest just smiled and said, "Work hard, and say a prayer for me." Two weeks later, Monsignor died. Little Joe was his last recommendation. On June 16, Little Joe was working labor for $1.19 an hour. On August 1, all basic steel mills in the country were on strike for 116 days. Little Joe and over a million other Steelworkers were out of a job.

Little Joe shook his head and cussed, "Come on, lights, damn it! You would think these people would let someone cross the street!"

Determined and pissed, he stepped off the curb. It was a Nippon car that hit him first. It threw him up in the air and over the roof of the car with its tinted sunroof in the open position. Little Joe looked down at the top of the perpetrator's bald head as he flew from there and bounced, not so gently, onto the hood of an American-made Chevrolet that passed him up and over its roof right into the shiny grill of a semi-truck that was carrying live chickens.

The semi was hardly moving because when the driver saw the old man flying through the air the first time round, he stepped hard on his air breaks, hissing almost to a complete stop—only to meet up with the poor guy on his just-polished, chrome grill.

All traffic came to a complete stop. Little Joe was now on his back in the middle of the street, bleeding. After he smacked the semi, he kind of slid down into a little heap. His legs were twisted and turned backwards underneath him. His limber, twisted body resembled a stringless marionette carelessly dropped in the middle of Indianapolis Boulevard. *Everything happened so fast*, Little Joe thought. It hurt like hell when he was first hit, then he couldn't feel a thing. It was like a bad movie in slow motion. It was crazy because he could see and hear people talking, but it sounded like they were talking in a barrel. He heard some idiot keep asking, "What happened? What happened?"

What the hell does he think happened? Little Joe thought. Then somebody placed a blanket under his head. *I don't need a damn pillow,* he wanted to say. He tried to tell everyone that he was OK; that everything was all right and he was just banged up a bit. But he couldn't formulate the words. Some kind soul walked up and very gently placed his hand-carved, ivory-handled ebony cane next to him. Little Joe heard some young fuck say, "Damn, I'm going to be late for work!"

That son of a bitch, he's worried he's going to be late, and I'm laying in the street all fucked up! Don't he know that damn mill ain't going nowhere, he wanted to shout.

And then he looked up and noticed the street lights. They were working. Little Joe smiled and closed his eyes. That's when he saw his wife.

She leaned down with her arms open and whispered, "Let's go home, Joe—I love you."

He reached out his hand and said, "It's been a long time, baby. I love you too."

Who the Hell Are You?

Gary Markley

Oh shit! Just what I needed to happen. Why can't they make these damn faucets work the same? One quarter turn at home and the water comes out just fine. One quarter turn here and it's a fire hose splashing down the front of my dress pants. Now it looks like I pissed all over myself. I hate this damn suit. I promised myself I wouldn't wear this thing again til I was buried in it.

Damn these worthless paper towels! They aren't doing any good at all! This wet spot is going to draw everyone's attention to my fly. Now I have to walk out and say, "That's right everyone, I peed my pants. Ha ha ha . . . ." God dammit.

Where's that damn comb? Why am I playing hide and seek with myself? Jesus, Stew! Put the comb back in the same pocket, dumbass! I must be losing it like my brother says. I'm definitely losing the old carpet. Hell, it only takes five strokes to comb it now. And look at this shit—another three hairs gave up and joined the comb.

Look at my eyes. I remember when Terre and I started dating, she said I had the most fascinating eyes. They look so faded now. And seem permanently bloodshot. My fat eyelids have slipped down over my eyes. I look so tired and old.

I remember Ed Teal's fifty-fifth birthday when he told Dan Scott and me that birthdays just don't excite him any more. He said his new definition of happiness was having a solid bowel movement when he woke up. I thought he was a disgusting old man then. I should have listened to the voice of experience. Hell, I have to eat the fiber equivalent of a potato sack to stay regular now.

I used to drink twelve beers and dance all night in bars and never once have to piss. I would go home and shoot a solid stream from five feet away into the toilet. I could write my name and the preamble to the Constitution in the snow with my dick. After all the years of fun we've had together, and now it just hangs there like it doesn't even know me.

Maybe if I had a decent hand I wouldn't have this problem. This hand is just as withered as my Johnson. Who knows what would be different if I didn't have to have this useless hand. I bet it would have changed everything, I probably wouldn't even be here right now .

"On this next coil I'll do the loading and you thread it up, OK?" My trainee seemed to be slow in catching on with the equipment.

"Yeah, OK," the trainee said.

"You know what to do, right?"

"Uhhh . . . sort of."

"Watch this time," I said. "I'll show you again. Turn this handle to the left, and the rolls open up. I'll feed the end of the strip between them and then raise my arm up to give you the OK sign. If the strip is bent and won't slide in, I'll raise my arm to give you the stop or hold it sign. I'll cut off the end till it's straight and try again to load it. When I give you the OK sign you turn the same handle to the right and it will close the rolls down on the strip. Then you push this button to move the strip along to the welding section, OK?"

"Got it," he said.

Got it, my ass, I thought to myself. Somehow I always got stuck with the new guys. I had only been at the mill four years myself and I'd been stuck training the last two newcomers.

"Here we go. You ready?"

"Yep," he said.

"You know, you talk too much, fella," I said sarcastically as I headed for the next coil to load into the line. As I slid the strip in between the rolls, it caught on one side and it bent. Wouldn't you know it? The kid had been threading them up all night and hadn't bent a one. At least he'd get to see all the hand signals when I fixed the problem.

I reached in with my left hand to pull out the strip and raised my right arm to give the "stop" or "hold" sign.

It happened just the way I've heard people say it does—in super slow motion. I heard the hydraulics lock in. I saw the 15-inch shiny silver rolls come together and swallow my hand. Then I heard the crack of bones as they were being crushed. I felt the skin of my fingertips split open. Blood shot out like ketchup packets that have been stomped on.

It took a second for the pain to set in. Then it came like a freight train. Later people told me they've never heard a human scream like I did.

It seemed to take the trainee minutes to turn the handle to release me. When he finally did, I went down to the floor. My only saving grace was that I quickly passed out from the shock. When I regained consciousness, it was behind a curtain of heavy drugs. I heard my brother and my wife. They just looked like opaque objects to me when I opened my eyes.

My wife told me I was heading to surgery soon. I asked if she had seen my hand. She said no and refused to look. My brother told me he had talked to a doctor and he said it looked like I was going to lose the hand.

"Don't do it!" I shouted. "Don't you let them do it! I don't want a hook! I want a hand dammit!"

I made my brother swear he would order the doctors to save my hand, no matter how damaged it was. I cried all the way to the operating room thinking my life was over.

✦ ✦ ✦

"Hey, Stew, your wife sent me in to see if you fell in."

Jesus! Can't a guy get a little privacy?

"Stop shinning the pole and get out here, dude!"

"That you, Tom?"

"Yeah. What are you doing, taking a nap?"

"Guess so. I'll be out soon."

"Hurry up, Stew. Wendy the new tractor driver came in. You know, the one who makes the simple act of breathing an art form?"

"OK, OK. I'm coming!"

I should have taken a hook or an artificial hand. But no. I asked for this worthless thing. Thank God for Terre. Man the months of putting up with me trying to deal with this hand. Look at you, you worthless piece of shit. You can't shake hands, help me pull up my pants, tuck in my shirt, or hold a cup of water. You can't even just hang there. You make me look like a freak.

I worked like a dog to return to work and what did I get? Three days off without pay for performing an unsafe act. Welcome back, Stewart. I didn't expect an award, but that was truly a surprise.

"Come on, Don, you can't take me off the line. These are the guys I've worked with for years!"

"I'm sorry, Stew, but they feel you just can't handle the requirements of the job," my boss said.

"I'll take a cut in pay and I'll work overtime to finish anything that I was supposed to do, Don. But you can't take me off the line!"

"It's not my call, Stew—just my job to tell you."

"This is bullshit, Don! You know why they want me off the line—so your boss Gaston can put his kid on the line!"

"You don't know that."

"Then you promise me that he won't be my replacement."

"I can't do that. He just might have the years to get your job."

"Hell, you and I both know he does. They've been trying to figure out how to get me off the line for three years so Junior can get my job. I gave my hand for this company, Don! Don't I deserve better than being dropped at a desk to shuffle papers around til I leave?"

"Stewart, they made the call, not me."

"They? They? Who are THEY anyway? Every time something bad has to be done to us workers you guys say, 'THEY did it, not us. We didn't take your cost of living raises away, THEY did. We didn't want to lower your incentive last year, THEY did.' Funny how you know I'm responsible for my injury."

Son of a bitch! I got water on my pants again! You're supposed to be happy today, Stew. Stop getting worked up by rehashing the past. Think about something else. Like, where in the hell did those wrinkles come from? I don't mind laugh crinkles, but these look like they're a quarter-inch deep. They're like damn canyons running the length of my face!

When did I get too small for my skin? I got a neck like a turkey! The only place where the skin is tight is around my nose. My whole life I've hated my big nose and now it's the only part of my body that looks the same as it did when I was younger. And Jesus Christ! When did I start growing hair out of my ears? Damn, when I tilt my head down, the extra skin on my throat hangs over my shirt collar.

Who did this to you, Stew? You don't look like this! If I take my hand and pull it hard across here I might be able to . . . There he is! That kinda looks like the kid who joined the mill years ago.

"Hey, you! Yeah, you, pretty boy, what's your name?"

"Stewart."

"Well, Stewart, you got hundreds of hours of probationary time before you get to be one of us, so you better keep your nose clean and do what I say. Judging by your nose, you're gonna to have to work hard. Ha ha ha ha!"

"I will," I said, thinking he was an asshole.

"Follow me then."

Follow him? I was right on top of him. Everything about that place scared me. The noises were unbearable. The floor was slick as ice. Hundreds of vehicles and machines were banging, clanking, beeping, crunching, whistling, humming, and screeching. There were sparks of electricity and machinery spinning so fast it made me dizzy. The welding areas where two steel coils get joined threw large amounts of sparks in the air. Machinery was moving on the ceiling, all around me, even in the basement.

I became part of the traffic jam on the mill floor in my first month when I learned to drive a forklift tractor. I was a laborer in the tin temper mill area. Everyone loved to needle the new guys. I took my share of abuse for my "pretty boy" status. I learned to ignore their snide remarks. Besides, I had style. I kept my Afro looking good, which was hard when you wear a helmet. My bellbottoms were neatly pressed and I had American-flag fringe on the cuffs. I had the hip big collars and I always got attention when I wore my big eagle medallion and turquoise peace-sign rings made by authentic Indian artisans. What was funny was the tiny little fifties sideburns those guys were hanging onto.

Now I look like shit. But at least I smell good. I shaved today and slapped on some Stetson. How long have I been in this damn bathroom anyway? Fifteen minutes? Why am I even wearing this watch? I got it five years ago. My "special gift" from my "grateful company" for 25 years of faithful service. Twenty-five goddamn years and they send a watch to my house. No handshake. No announcement. No thank-you. Why would they? I haven't been an asset to them. I'm a damn liability.

It took them some years to finally eliminate all of the job openings for someone with my seniority. I got my 30 years in, so I guess I can't complain. My friends and family, along with some poor guy in management who has to pretend he likes me, have gathered to celebrate my retirement.

I got lots of nice presents. Had a good meal. Told a lot of stories. Now they're waiting for me to come out and give my farewell address. But I don't want to leave! I've been forced out. What am I supposed to do now? I want to work! I don't want to sit in a rocker til I die! I don't want to hear how lucky I am to not have to work. What else is a man supposed to do? When you go, so do the friends you worked with for years. You don't have anything in common any more. They drift away.

This isn't fair! Everyone will forget me . . . except the company. That'll change when I finally die and they can officially close the book on me. Stop it, Stew! You're wife and kids are waiting on you.

I'll find something to do. Yeah, right! Maybe I'll just wander the beach in my Bermuda shorts and black socks with black wingtips like a loser. Is this it? This is all I get for a lifetime of effort? This is what I get for losing a hand, and more importantly, my youth?

Pull it together now, Stew! Straighten the tie. Wipe away the tears you sissy. Button the coat up. One last look. My God. Who the hell are you? What's your name?

I push the bathroom door open and trudge toward the banquet table. "Here he is everybody!" the sound system blares. "The man of the hour, Mr. Retirement himself . . . Stewart Simmons!"

Outside Looking In

J.A. Orellana

A baby-face walking
alongside the barbed wire fences wraps his eyes around the
prickling red,
dull, silvery carcass, belching fiery breaths from the churning mill,
and wonders what it's like inside.
Hard-faced, mill rats with steel orbs trickle out
then flood out
the clock-house gate:
Exodus at torrent speed in a rush to escape from
what? To where?
And he wonders what it's like
inside.
Shoveling coal and churning out
structural T's.
A good meal ticket at the price of 10 years
off your life.
And he wonders what it's like inside.

Missing At Work

Joe E. Gutierrez

Pushing the wheelbarrow up the mound that surrounded the cast-iron mold took every bit of strength he had. The giant, smoke-filled building where he labored, with its bent, burnt-out eyes rusted shut, stood there on the black edge of the lake, angry and mean, laughing quietly, hot summer after hot summer.

It held him and other workers like him prisoner with its rotten-egg smelling, graphite-filled air that wrapped itself around man and machine alike and just laid there like a spent two-dollar whore who just didn't care anymore. This "steel mill" was a city within a city where 25,000 Steelworkers lived, worked and died making steel around the clock, seven days a week for a dollar nineteen an hour.

The dirty, black smoke pushed itself up and out of the molten steel, making it difficult to breathe. This was the only source of light and it hit him in blinding staccato flashes, making his job even more difficult. Balancing the wheelbarrow on the narrow planks that led to the edge of the hot mold was a test of endurance that would have made his father proud. His father pounded a work ethic into his head that wore around his neck like an anvil, constantly reminding him of his responsibilities as a man. He could still hear him say, "When someone pays you good money to work, you must work! If you don't want to work, get out! There's always someone else who can take your place."

His father died years ago in Mexico, but he was still alive in him and in every iron pellet in that wheelbarrow and in every drop of sweat that fell to the ground. Yes! It was a matter of pride to reach the top of the mountain without losing a pellet.

Jose Rubio was working the midnight shift in the Open Hearth. It was July, and the heat was suffocating. Desperately trying to keep the wheelbarrow on the wooden planks, his thoughts flashed back to the recurring nightmare that plagued his sleep. It was always the same. Even now he could feel the cold fear and pain that he felt as he saw himself falling into a cauldron of molten steel. His body would disappear moments before he touched the searing heat; moments before his scream jolted him awake. The last few times were the worst, because he knew he was awake. At least he thought he was awake, then prayed that he was asleep. When he opened his eyes, he could see and hear, but couldn't move. He opened his mouth to cry for help, but no sound would come. He was on fire and he was all alone and he hurt. God! How it hurt! When he finally scared himself awake, he couldn't go back to sleep. He didn't want to go back to sleep. The dreams sucked the strength out of him and left him tired and depleted like an old washer woman, bitter and barren; a woman who never knew the pleasures of love and a gentle hand.

Today he was pushing a bigger load than usual. The lack of sleep and weight pulling on his arms and legs was taking a toll. He felt as if his arms were being pulled out of their sockets and his legs were like water. Sweat poured down his back. He had worked for hours without a break. He had seen no one since the beginning of the shift. He usually enjoyed working by himself. It gave him time to think. But anymore, he didn't like to work alone. Those damn dreams made him nervous.

As he neared the top of the mound, a sudden blast of radiant heat blasted his face, forcing him to quickly turn his head. Two feet from the edge of the fire, he felt the wheel slip off the board. He pushed the handles to the right, but to no avail. And just like in his dream, as if in slow motion, he began to fall. Stubbornly, he refused to let go of the wheelbarrow. He had worked too hard, and after all, it was a matter of pride. There was no time to scream as he fell into the molten steel. Jose could see his wife and children as he followed his nemesis into the fire. He suddenly released his hold, but it was too late—his hands pushed into and parted the flaming liquid, making way for the rest of his body. The molten steel closed quietly over Jose Rubio, leaving only the stench of his burned flesh, which immediately mingled with the captured breath of this wretched building. Jose Rubio became one with it all, and to look for a trace of him on the molten surface would have been futile.

Eight hours later, another worker trudged up the narrow path trying not to spill a pellet. After all, it was a matter of pride.

A Violet in the Light
Dwight "Doc" Iler

As I walked around my office performing my daily tasks, I thought about the journey that ultimately brought me to this place and this position. I mean, here I was—a nice, clean work environment—a place totally new to me. I was accustomed to working in the dirty, greasy, noisy mills for years, and it was in my blood. Now after a long, hard journey I found myself in a better place, working in a training program for Steelworkers. I realized that sometimes adversity and hardship mark the beginning of a successful journey. As I adjusted the window blinds in my office, I saw my African Violets straining forward to grab every bit of the warm, radiant light that danced through the window and I realized just how refreshing and necessary that light is. My mind raced back to my journey, which began in a cold, dark place.

It was 1983, and I was perched on a stool in the middle of a cold, dark building. As I looked through the very dim lighting, I saw nothing but gigantic holes in the concrete floor from where machinery had been dug up, and a huge void that just seemed to swallow up everything. I thought to myself, "I've got to get out of this dark place." You see this wasn't the place that I once knew. The place I once knew was vibrant and full of life. I remembered the loud banging sound of 16-inch diameter pipe as it came off the mill, lumbered down the washout table, and banged into the piece of pipe in front of it. I recalled the whirring sound of the threader and coupler machines and the squeal of the pipe as its ends were beveled and threaded. The occasional boom of a defective weld as it exploded while being pressure tested. The noise used to be so loud that I had to wear ear protection to work here or risk losing my hearing. The only thing that I could hear at that moment was the deafening silence, and then the sound of a camera shutter clicking and reverberating through the entire building. In the midst of a sweeping wave of anxiety, I said to myself, "I gotta get out of this dark place."

I left my stool and weakly dragged myself over by the doorway. There was a hint of sunlight coming through the shaded doorway. And, like that African Violet, I wanted it. I looked out onto the parking lot where hundreds of cars were once parked. There were just two cars there now. One car was my 1979 Oldsmobile 98—gold with a black vinyl top—still looking like new. The other was a little white vehicle. I believe it was foreign made, and it had writing on the side that said "U. S. News and World Report."

"This lot always had been full of cars . . ." I said to myself, ". . . Just isn't right."

A young photographer prowled around the place seeking a good place to take his snapshots. He was a young man, in jeans, probably fresh out of college. He seemed impervious to the sounds and sights that I experienced. After all, how could he know?

"Turn just a little this way," he said. I swung around on the stool to face him. I heard the sound of the camera shutter and a bright light flashed in my eyes. It left dots before my eyes, flashing like the sparks that cascaded from the welder's rod as he repaired the equipment, or the sparks that leapt from the burner's torch as he cut out samples. Then the spots faded and I wondered, "How can such light live in this dark place?"

The female reporter circled around the area, peering into corners as if seeking lost treasure. The sound of her high heels as they clicked on the concrete floor was well out of place. Greasy, steel-toed metatarsal work shoes had once graced this floor.

Out of the darkness I heard her say, "How many people used to work here?"

"Eight hundred," I answered in a voice that cracked with the weight of despair that pressed upon it.

"You think they'll find work?"

"It'll never compare to what we're losing, but we'll make it . . . we're survivors," I responded.

My mind raced to the people that once helped give life to this place. Almost every one of them had become part of my extended family. This group trusted me to represent them, and sometimes, to protect them. They elected me as their shop steward, alternate zone man, and ultimately, the zone man. For 11 years I worked with these people. I cried when their kids got hurt and celebrated when they graduated. I ate at their table and they ate at mine. When I had problems, my extended family was there to see me through, and when they had problems, I was there. After a long day, a bunch of us would sometimes get together, go to the local joint, and get juiced—"Just washing down the steel dust," we'd say. But today the bunch can't be found.

I thought about Saturday. I received an early morning Saturday phone call that said, "Sit down, Doc, got something to tell you. You know Bill— we were with him at the union hall yesterday—his wife called me this morning. He blew his brains out last night. And the young guy, Steve, from the shipping floor—last week his wife found him hanging in the basement."

This thing really affected me . . . it plain and simple messed me up. I remember thinking to myself, "How could this happen? How did I let this happen? I should have seen it coming and intervened. Boy, I've gotta get outta this dark place—this place, it makes you do crazy stuff."

The reporter continued to ask questions, but I can't even tell you what those questions were. They just sounded like so much prattle in my ears at the time. After a moment of staring, and watching the ghosts of days past here, I heard the voice behind me say, "Well, looks like this interview is all done, Doc. What are you going to do now that the mill is shut down? Where to now?"

"Don't know," I replied, "but with help from the Lord, I'll land on my feet."

I walked out of that dank, dark, shut-down pipe mill with the reporter and photographer that day. The sunlight was so bright it hurt my eyes. I put on my shades and pondered whether or not this was a good time to go get juiced. As I drove off, I knew that I had begun a journey to I knew not where. The only thing I knew was that I had to get away from that place.

As I pointed my gold and black Oldsmobile 98 toward the security gate, I looked back at the empty, quiet parking lot. I looked at the building, now lifeless, so dark and cold-looking. The place that once provided a valuable product to the public, and was a means of provision for many working families, now lay as a place where the birds congregate to find quietness in this industrial haven. I came to the gate and waved goodbye to the security guard. I had seen this guy around for years. As I waved to him, I thought to myself, "This will be the last time, pal. I'm leaving this dark place." That was the day that, just like the African Violet, I started reaching for all the sunlight I could get.

Cedar Hill Publications

SET THIS BOOK ON FIRE!—*Jimmy Santiago Baca*
$15—Poetry   ISBN: 1-891812-23-8
(Order from Endeavor Books @ 888/324-9303 Toll Free)

THE HEAT: *Steelworker Lives and Legends*
$15—Prose & Poetry   ISBN: 1-891812-17-3

AMNESIA TANGO—*Alan Britt*
$10—Poetry   ISBN: 1-891812-14-9

AMERICAN MINOTAUR—*Leonard J. Cirino*
$9—Poetry ISBN: 1-891812-22-X

96 SONNETS FACING CONVICTION—*Leonard J. Cirino*
$10—Poetry   ISBN: 1-891812-20-3

THE TERRIBLE WILDERNESS OF SELF—*Leonard J. Cirino*
$10—Poetry   ISBN:1-891812-00-9

SUBURBAN LIGHT—*William Doreski*
$10—Poetry   ISBN: 1-891812-16-5

BODY AND SOUL—*Sharon Doubiago*
$15—Poetry   ISBN: 1-891812-24-6
(Order from Endeavor Books @ 888/324-9303 Toll Free)

THE SILK AT HER THROAT—*James Doyle*
$10—Poetry   ISBN: 1-891812-12-4

NEXT EXIT—*Taylor Graham*
$10—Poetry   ISBN: 1-891812-13-0

7th CIRCLE—*Maggie Jaffe*
$10—Poetry   ISBN: 1-891812-07-6

THE PRISONS—*Maggie Jaffe*
$15—Poetry   ISBN: 1-891812-21-1

WHITHER AMERICAN POETRY—*Michael McIrvin*
$14—Critical Essays   ISBN: 1-891812-26-2

THE BOOK OF ALLEGORY—*Michael McIrvin*
$10—Poetry   ISBN:1-891812-03-3

PROVERBS FOR THE INITIATED—*Kenn Mitchell*
$11—Poetry   ISBN: 1-891812-06-8

1917—*Joe Napora*
$10.00—Poetry   ISBN: 1-891812-18-1

BRAMBLECROWN—*Georgette Perry*
$5—Poetry ISBN: 1-891812-25-4

GRAY AIR—*Christopher Presfield*
$8—Poetry ISBN: 1-891812-15-7

GUTTERSNIPE CANTICLE—*Amelia Raymond*
$9—Poetry ISBN: 1-891812-22-X

"EDEN, OVER . . ."—*Tim Scannell*
$5—Poetry ISBN:1-891812-01-7

dot.bomb—*Deborah Small*
$15—Art & Prose   ISBN: 1-891812-09-2

SOME SORT OF JOY—*John Taylor*
$15—PROSE   ISBN: 1-891812-08-4

THE WORLD AS IT IS—*John Taylor*
$10—Prose ISBN: 1-891812-04-1

ILLUSION JUNKIE DOWNTOWN—*Chocolate Waters*
$15—Poetry   (forthcoming)

AMERIKA / AMERICA—*Marilyn Zuckerman*
$15—Poetry   ISBN: 891812-10-0

PIECES OF EIGHT: *A Women's Anthology of Verse*
$10—Poetry   ISBN:1-891812-02-5

JAM: *Cedar Hill Anthology Series*
$10—Poetry   ISBN: 1-891812-05-X